LENTEN GRACE

LENTEN GRACE

Daily Gospel Reflections

By the Daughters of Saint Paul

BOOKS & MEDIA
Boston

Library of Congress Cataloging-in-Publication Data

Lenten grace : daily Gospel reflections / by the Daughters of Saint Paul.
    p. cm.
  ISBN 0-8198-4525-6 (pbk.)
  1. Lent—Prayers and devotions. 2. Catholic Church—Prayers and devotions.
3. Bible N.T. Gospels—Meditations. I. Daughters of St. Paul.
  BX2170.L4L47 2008
  242'.34—dc22

                        2008025737

Cover design by Rosana Usselmann

Cover photo: Mary Emmanuel Alves, FSP

Interior photos: Armanda L. Santos, FSP, and Mary Emmanuel Alves, FSP, © Daughters of St. Paul

Published by Pauline Books & Media, 50 Saint Paul's Avenue, Boston, MA 02130-3491

Printed in the U.S.A.

www.pauline.org

Pauline Books & Media is the publishing house of the Daughters of St. Paul, an international congregation of women religious serving the Church with the communications media.

1 2 3 4 5 6 7 8 9   12 11 10 09 08

Contents

How to Use This Book

:· · · · · · · · · · · · ·:

"Speak, LORD, for your servant is listening" (1 Sam 3:9).

Lent is a "favorable time" (cf. Is 49:8), a time of abundant grace that draws us toward God and away from the darkness of sin.

In these pages, various members of the Daughters of St. Paul share moments of joy and insight through prayer with Scripture. Our Founder, Blessed James Alberione, encouraged such prayer, saying, "The person who nourishes himself or herself on the Word of the Bible ... will be penetrated by the Holy Spirit." The Word of God presented to us in the liturgy during Lent is especially rich and favorable to deeper prayer and contemplation.

Following the Gospel reading for each day of Lent, these reflections are based on *Lectio Divina* ("holy reading"), which is a way of praying with Scripture. Many methods of doing this have developed since the time of early monasticism. Here, the sisters use a simple framework that allows the Word of God to make room in our minds and hearts.

The first step, *Lectio* ("reading"), is to read the day's Gospel passage from a missal or Bible. Read it a few times slowly, perhaps especially noticing the phrase or verse that is listed under the *Meditatio* section.

Next, the *Meditatio* ("meditation") expands the meaning of this phrase and explores what it is saying to us today—what

God is asking of us, or challenging us to, or offering to us. After reading the meditation, take as much time as you like to reflect on it.

The *Oratio* ("prayer") can help you talk to God about what has arisen in your heart, so that the time of prayer becomes a conversation, not just a time to think. God has spoken in the Scripture. We hear the invitation in our meditation, but now a response is called for. Our response is not just to say, "Yes, I want to do as you are asking me," but also to say, "Help me do it, Lord!"

The short line under *Contemplatio* ("contemplation") is a way of extending this time of prayer into life. You can silently repeat it throughout the day to help deepen the intimacy with the Lord that you experienced in prayer.

May your Lent be grace-filled and abundantly blessed!

Liturgical Calendar

∴ ⋯⋯⋯⋯ ∴

Note to the reader: The weekday readings during Lent are the same from year to year, but the Sunday readings follow a three-year cycle (A, B, or C) as indicated in the following chart:

Year	Cycle
2009	Cycle B
2010	Cycle C
2011	Cycle A
2012	Cycle B
2013	Cycle C
2014	Cycle A
2015	Cycle B
2016	Cycle C
2017	Cycle A
2018	Cycle B
2019	Cycle C
2020	Cycle A
2021	Cycle B
2022	Cycle C

Come out to the desert,
that place of silence and patience.
Come listen to the voice of God.

Ash Wednesday

∴ ⋯⋯⋯ ∴

Lectio

Matthew 6:1–6, 16–18

Meditatio

"... [Do not] perform righteous deeds in order that people may see them ... your Father who sees in secret will repay you."

"What are you going to do for Lent?" As children each year we had to answer this question. We gave up cookies, candy, TV, video games...; the list was made up of our most precious pleasures. We struggled through the forty days of Lent, flexing our spiritual muscles as we raced toward the Easter Day finish line. As adults we've settled into a more sophisticated Lenten spirituality, but often we end up giving up the same things we did as kids, perhaps hoping to lose a little weight or gain a little time.

Today's Gospel reading prods us to go deeper. It centers around theatrics. We all are mini-celebrities of our own lives, imagining a trail of adoring fans following us. We can even make Lent into a minor Hollywood production. We conceive the idea for our Lenten penance. We write the script. We are producer, director, actor, and audience all wrapped in one. And we end up at the Easter Day finish line as self-absorbed as we were on Ash Wednesday.

Perhaps these words of Jesus spoken to us today are asking us to go backstage, take the last seat, sit down, and wait for God to reveal to us the script he has written for us this Lent. Perhaps as adults we should be asking at the beginning of Lent: What is God going to do for me in these next forty days? What is it that I desire God to do for me in this long Lenten retreat?

Instead of theatrics, Jesus is inviting us to simple honesty. To smallness. To just being there and sensing his grace, quiet enough, still enough to feel the gentle tugs of the Spirit to newness, to giving up obstacles to the growth of a treasured relationship, to finding a few moments daily to read the Word of God, to surrender fear.... What God is going to do in your life will surprise you. Expect it.

Oratio

Jesus, I am not accustomed to telling you to do whatever you want in my life. In fact, it's kind of scary to see what you would do if I let you write my life's script. I think I am doing a pretty good job at my life on my own. But it seems you want something more of me now. Instead of Lent being *my* focus, you are placing me front and center in *your* focus. I am expecting you to show me what you want to give me at this stage of my life. I trust you.

Contemplatio

I expect you, God, to do something with me this Lent.

Thursday after Ash Wednesday

∴ ⋯⋯⋯ ∴

Lectio

Luke 9:22–25

Meditatio

> *"If anyone wishes to come after me, he must . . .*
> *take up his cross daily and follow me."*

Today's Gospel challenges us to true discipleship, to follow a Messiah who defies all our human expectations. In the verses immediately preceding today's Gospel, Jesus asks his disciples, ". . . who do you say that I am?" Peter replies, "The Messiah of God" (v. 20). In this context of Peter's confession of faith, Jesus defines the kind of Messiah he is, challenging Peter (and each of us) to a deeper faith. Jesus reminds us that he did not choose to come into our world in glory and triumph. Instead, he chose to come into the world as a suffering Messiah who would be rejected, killed, and raised on the third day.

Jesus calls his disciples to follow in his footsteps and to take up our cross *daily*. . . . That word "daily" stands out for me. Jesus is asking us for commitment—a resolute decision to carry our cross—not just through this season of Lent, or when big sufferings come our way, but *every day*. Yet how are we to do this?

For those of us seeking to live the Christian life, we won't have to look far to find the cross. We are called to *daily* lay down our lives by letting go of our own preferences, desires, strong opinions. We make choices for the sake of Christ and his Gospel and not on the basis of our own immediate feelings or reactions. On any given day, this may mean many things. Perhaps it will mean setting aside my own need for recognition while seeking to encourage others in their gifts, or choosing not to act out of feelings of anger when a family member says something that hurts. In each circumstance, we are called to choose Christ and to place the good of others before our own. Yet the cross never has the last word! With every death to self, the cross leads to resurrection and new life in Christ.

Oratio

Jesus, I do not always understand your ways. Sometimes, your cross feels like folly to me. Why would you choose suffering and death over triumph and glory? Teach me the mystery of your ways, and how to choose the good of others before my own. This Lent, I renew my commitment to carry my cross daily. May this laying down of my life unite me with you and bring life to others, allowing me to share more deeply in your Easter joy. For if I die with you, I will also live with you.

Contemplatio

"For to me, 'life' is Christ … " (Phil 1:21).

Friday after Ash Wednesday

Lectio

Matthew 9:14–15

Meditatio

"Can the wedding guests mourn as long as the bridegroom is with them?"

Today's reference to the bridegroom is one of many uses of marriage imagery in the Gospels. Jesus refers to himself as the "bridegroom" and tells a parable about a king who threw a wedding banquet for his son. In another passage, the familiar story of the wise and foolish virgins also centers on the arrival of the bridegroom. Those who were ready went in with him to celebrate the wedding feast. In John's Gospel the Baptist declares: "The one who has the bride is the bridegroom; the best man, who stands and listens for him, rejoices greatly at the bridegroom's voice. So this joy of mine has been made complete" (Jn 3:29). A major wedding connection is also made in the Gospel of John with the marriage feast at Cana, when Jesus turned water into wine. In the Old Testament we find the Song of Songs and, in the prophets, the heart-rending love God has for his people who turned away from him adulterously to follow false idols.

Augustine also used this nuptial imagery, speaking of Jesus' coming into the world in terms of marriage. For

Augustine this imagery of bride and bridegroom is a symbol of Jesus' spousal desire for us, his love that blindly gives itself over to union whatever the cost, the beginning of a love affair born in eternity, to be consummated on the marriage bed of the cross, and finally raised in glory to the right hand of the Father.

When disciples fast today, it is a fasting of faith because Jesus has ascended into heaven. More than the lack of food, it is the absence of the sight of the bridegroom. It is a continual search for him and a longing for his return. Fasting from food, from TV, from complaining, or whatever else we decide to fast from, is a discipline that helps us keep focused on why we are here: we are invited to a forever wedding feast, not simply as a guest, but as the bride.

Oratio

Jesus, when we could not come to you, you came to us to forge an unbreakable bond between us and God, a bond of love that will last for eternity. At the beginning of these days of penitence, I feel this bond strengthening. I feel that you care about me and my life. I feel that you want me to realize how close you are to me. Help me to let go of whatever habits have become obstacles to living in your presence.

Contemplatio

You have come into the world as to a marriage.

Saturday after Ash Wednesday

∴ ⋯⋯⋯⋯ ∴

Lectio

Luke 5:27–32

Meditatio

"Then Levi gave a great banquet for him in his house,
and a large crowd of tax collectors and others were at table with them."

Could I entertain Jesus in my house tonight? Who would
I invite? Who would just show up? Would I have the nerve—
or the courage—to call the usual crowd? Or would I try to
reinvent myself for this occasion? How long would I try to
sustain the act?

We sometimes say that God "takes us where we're at." Do
I truly come to prayer "as I am"? Do I allow the Lord into
the living room of my heart with all the inhabitants that have
taken up residence there? If I'm honest with myself I have to
admit that an odd assortment of people live in my memory.

There are, of course, the people whom I cherish and
whose lives are intertwined with my own: family members
and close friends. Near or far, living or deceased, these loved
ones live in my thoughts and prayers. It is good. On the other
hand, there are others, less welcome, who invade my imagination and memory. An unsightly assortment of ghosts and
skeletons clutter my mental landscape and distract me from

the conversation I wish to have with Jesus. Or do they? What would happen if I brought Jesus into the place where arguments, manipulation, and betrayals lurk and periodically replay themselves?

"Those who are healthy do not need a physician, but the sick do." To his credit, Levi invited Jesus to his house and introduced him to the people he typically sat down to dinner with. Other people murmured (of course), but Jesus came anyway and was perfectly at ease at Levi's table.

Perhaps I need an honest heart-to-heart with God about the people that I live with in the "real world" as well as those who populate my "inner world."

Oratio

Jesus, come into the house of my heart. Walk through the rooms of my mind: my memories, imagination, thoughts, and desires. Let us sit down together and chat for a while. I have so much to tell you—and so much I need to hear from you.

You and I both know the company I keep. Help me to leave behind relationships that are unhealthy. Help me to strengthen and heal those that need repair. You called Levi into the community of your disciples. Lord, introduce me to your friends, because in the end, I want always to be found in *your* company.

Contemplatio

"Those who are healthy do not need a physician, but the sick do."

Sunday of the First Week of Lent — A

∵ ·········· ∵

Lectio

Matthew 4:1–11

Meditatio

"Jesus was led by the Spirit ..."

We can relate in a very deep way with Jesus as he experiences something so familiar to us: temptation. In this moment of his life, outside of his passion, Jesus is portrayed at his weakest in his human state. Yet, his divinity is clearly manifested as well.

"[C]ommand that these stones become loaves of bread." We too are tempted to fill the physical hunger and desires we feel with all kinds of material things. Yet a certain hunger often expresses itself as physical need that can only be filled with God's Word, God's presence. One does not live on bread alone, but on every word that comes forth from the mouth of God.

"If you are the Son of God, throw yourself down. For it is written: 'He will command ...'" How often do we put words in God's mouth? "God will bless you if you ..." "It must be God's will ..." Or we might bargain with God: "I will give up ... if you do ... for me." In this way, we test God's love for us. We actually put limits on God's love and dictate to him. We tell him what we want him to do. You shall not put the Lord, your God, to the test.

"All these I shall give to you, if you will prostrate yourself and worship me." We often live in a world of "ifs." If only I won the lottery.... If only I had a better job.... If only I had become a.... We often imagine ourselves in situations other than those we actually live in. What expense we go through trying to make these fantasies a reality. Playing them over and over again in our minds, they may become the object of our worship. The Lord, your God, shall you worship and him alone shall you serve.

Oratio

Be with me in the desert, Spirit of God. Grant me the grace to allow myself to be led by you in the wilderness, where noises cease and nothing can distract me from my own demons. When everything I depend on to sustain me is taken away, may your word be the bread I seek. When I doubt my Father's love and put it to the test, renew my trust. When I want to escape the trials of my life by seeking a fantasy, help me instead to adore you. Thus may my desert become the place where, in facing my stark humanity, I find communion with you.

Contemplatio

"Speak, Lord, for your servant is listening."

Sunday of the First Week of Lent — B

∴ ⋯⋯⋯⋯ ∴

Lectio

Mark 1:12–15

Meditatio

> *"... and the angels ministered to him ..."*

Mark gives a very brief account of the temptation of Jesus. We do not get a list of temptations nor of Jesus' responses. The little detail we are given is that angels came to minister to him.

In the verse preceding this passage, the Father says to Jesus, "You are my beloved Son; with you I am well pleased" (v. 11). Jesus is the Son of God—Jesus is God. Does he really need help combating Satan? This verbal and spiritual battle is between God and Satan, yet the angels are present. We can assume that God the Father sent the angels, but why? It is not to fight Satan in Jesus' place, but simply to be with him during this time in the desert.

God's love for us is so great that we too have angels all around us—not just heavenly creatures, but people through whom God leads us into a closer relationship with him. Lent gives us the opportunity to reflect on the many ways God graces us each day, especially through the many people he sends to be our angels.

I am reminded of times of difficulties in my own life and the people who gathered around me. I received so much strength and comfort simply because I was accompanied. I could have easily dismissed their actions because they weren't doing great acts. No, they sat with me, listened to me pour out my heart, and/or prayed for me. From their simple acts of love, God's blessings and graces have reached me.

As countless others have ministered to us, we can ask God for the grace to be open to go to the people that he wishes to send us to as messengers of his love. Just as the angels were sent by God to minister to Jesus, God sends us to minister to Jesus in all we do for our brothers and sisters.

Oratio

Lord, each day your love touches me through the people I come into contact with. Help me today to see these angels of yours and to be grateful for the many ways that you reach out to tell me of your great love for me through them. Help me to grow in gratitude of heart as well as in the desire and ability to serve you by serving others. What ways are you asking me to be your hands, voice, and heart in my daily life? Give me the grace to be open to your invitations today and throughout this Lenten journey.

Contemplatio

"This is the time of fulfillment ..."

Sunday of the First Week of Lent — C

❖ ⋯⋯⋯⋯ ❖

Lectio

Luke 4:1–13

Meditatio

> *"Jesus . . . was led by the Spirit . . . to be tempted."*

We can imagine Jesus going into the desert for his forty-day retreat, precious days of solitude with his Father. It is not surprising that the tempter took this opportunity to try his wiles on him. After all, Paul tells us, Jesus experienced all that we do except sin. It is a relief to know this, and it encourages us to imitate Jesus as we, too, experience temptations. Temptations are opportunities to make choices.

In our effort to imitate Jesus, it can be very helpful to prayerfully identify those opportunities we might encounter today or during this week. They can range from small to life-altering choices. Perhaps we struggle to be kind or patient with a particular person or are dealing with an illness. Maybe we worry about our family or finances or find it difficult to live our values in our workplace, home, or neighborhood. If everything seems to be "going our way," perhaps we find it difficult to remember to pray or to depend on God.

Whichever "opportunities for choices" arise during our day, we seek to imitate Jesus, who allowed the Spirit to lead him. What an encouragement it is to know that we are not alone in making our choices! The Spirit leads *us* too!

How can we recognize the Spirit's lead? The fruit of the Spirit is love, joy, peace … (cf. Gal 5:22). As we consider a choice, we cast an inward gaze at the feelings that arise. Is there an inner peace? This may signify the Spirit's invitation. Is there instead a feeling of restlessness or discontent? This choice is not inspired by the Spirit, and so we consider other options. In all our opportunities to make choices, we are blessed to know that the Spirit leads us and enables us to respond as Jesus did.

Oratio

Jesus, you were led by the Spirit into the desert and enlightened and strengthened by the Spirit when you encountered temptations. I do not know what choices I will need to make today and during this week. Please walk with me. Help me to be open to however the Spirit is leading me. Enable me to recognize which choices are invitations from the Spirit. Obtain for me the love, courage, and trust that I will need to say yes to each invitation as you did. I ask all of this in your name. Amen.

Contemplatio

The Spirit leads me as I encounter opportunities to make choices.

Monday of the First Week of Lent

⁝ ・・・・・・・・・・ ⁝

Lectio

Matthew 25:31–46

Meditatio

> *"Lord, when did we see you hungry ...*
> *and not minister to your needs?"*

Thoughts of the Last Judgment can be upsetting and downright frightening. We tend to concentrate too much on the idea of great destruction, whereas Jesus seeks to calm us with this simple description found in Matthew's Gospel. It is Discipleship 101. It is also a sneak preview of the most important test we will ever take, the ultimate placement test. Whether we are accepted into God's kingdom or banished from it eternally will depend on our answers to this test. We won't be able to read over another's shoulder or write hints on our hands. That is because we will have already written our answers prior to appearing before the Lord.

As we stand there in his presence he sees the answers written on our soul. Nevertheless, questions are still exchanged. We ask: "But when?" And Jesus will firmly reply: "When I was hungry, thirsty, sick, alone, in prison, and you came to me and cared for me. All that I expected of you as my disciple was this unconditional love for each person you met."

Jesus will not question us about the myriad matters that fill our waking hours and sleepless nights. He will not ask if we were successful, if we maintained our youthfulness or our enthusiasm for life. He will not even ask us if we prayed. He will not have to ask that because it will be evident by the God-likeness of our actions. And so, we listen attentively as he speaks to us each day: "You are to be one with me in heart and soul, to act as I act, to love as I love. Your love and energy need to be directed toward our Father in heaven, and this can be done best by sincerely caring about others, especially the stranger and the needy. Remember that when you do it for the least of my brothers and sisters, you do it for me."

Oratio

Jesus, give me a heart like your own. Help me always to recognize my daily opportunities to minister to you in the neediness of others. But even more, let me see the importance of every person on his or her own merit. Let me say to myself: *I want to help this person, my brother or sister, without any thought of a reward or even a kind word from my Lord.* I want to serve as you served, my Lord, for the ultimate good of each person. Strengthen and guide me today. Amen.

Contemplatio

Love me in those who share each day with you.

Tuesday of the First Week of Lent

∴ ⋯⋯⋯ ∴

Lectio

Matthew 6:7–15

Meditatio

> *"Forgive us our debts …"*

Much of Matthew's version of the Our Father and its sur-rounding context is devoted to forgiveness. After concluding the prayer, Jesus tells us that if we forgive we will be forgiv-en. A few verses earlier in this Gospel, he states that his Father makes the sun shine on the bad and good, the rain fall on the just and unjust—with no distinction. And he calls us to be merciful, as his Father is merciful.

Throughout the Gospels, we see God's mercy active in the person of Jesus, who forgives sins, delivers people from their afflictions, and socializes with the marginalized. In recent times—thanks to Saint Faustina and Pope John Paul II—the Church has grown in its appreciation of the depth of God's mercy. In fact, the Church sees mercy as the core of the Christian message.

Forgiveness can be heroic, as was Jesus' forgiveness of everyone responsible for his death. Many of Christ's follow-ers have likewise forgiven great wrongs. Just one example from our own times is Immaculée Ilibagiza, a Rwandan woman who forgave the neighbors who had massacred her parents and siblings. You and I may not be called to such heroism, but the Lord may be inviting us to accept acquaintances and even relatives whose values seem contrary to our own and thus foreign to the Gospel. That's often hard to do. But who knows what graces we may draw if we make a real effort to accept them as persons loved by God?

Then there are the wrongs done to us personally, such as slander, gossip, digs, slights.... These might actually seem easier to forgive, since we could take pride in our "virtue." Perhaps real virtue is cultivated by putting up with the *little* grievances that are not sins, yet get on our nerves. A spouse, friend, colleague, or sibling may persist in an irritating habit that we've called to their attention. What if we were to focus on that person's good qualities and forget about the irritation?

Oratio

Jesus, help me to recognize that we're all children of your heavenly Father—one human family in need of mercy. Help me try to see where my companions are coming from and what they're going through. May I forgive as you did, who ate and drank with sinners, and as your Father does, who showers sunshine and rain on all alike. Make me blind to irritating faults. Let me see something of your own goodness in each person I live with, work with, or meet.

Contemplatio

"... as we forgive our debtors."

Wednesday of the First Week of Lent

∴ ⋯⋯⋯⋯⋯ ∴

Lectio

Luke 11:29–32

Meditatio

"This generation ... seeks a sign."

A sign is something that points to another reality. For example, the letter H on a blue rectangle indicates a hospital nearby. Lent has its own signs: ashes, purple vestments, absent Glorias, and buried alleluias.

In the novel *Brideshead Revisited*, a priest at the bedside of a dying sinner asks him to give some sign of his repentance. Unable to speak, the dying man traces a large sign of the cross over his chest. As he does so, all in the room fall to their knees. That sign speaks of hope and repentance.

Jesus mentions Jonah, the reluctant prophet. God asked Jonah to go and preach in Nineveh, but Jonah balked and fled. Then he was swallowed by a large fish. Scholars may point out that the Jonah story is an allegory—a sort of parable meant to show the Israelites, and us, that God does not reserve his love for only one kind of people. He wants all to repent and be saved from destruction, even the non-Jewish Ninevites.

I was fascinated by a marine science book that pictured a whale-sized grouper. Grouper fish do not bite but almost inhale or gulp their food. The book said that this eating style could explain how the story of Jonah might possibly be factual. Whether allegory or not, Jonah's sign of being hidden, truly buried in the sea in the fish's belly, paints a vivid picture of how much Jesus loves us. Jesus' body will be hidden away in the tomb—out of sight just like Jonah. After three days he will rise and signal to all that he is truly God. This Jesus who rose from the tomb draws us out of the grouper bellies we may use to hide our "specialty," that little or big sin that keeps us from basking in the light of Christ's constant love for us.

Oratio

Lord Jesus, thank you for the enormous sign of your resurrection and the dying and rising that I experience in the sacrament of Reconciliation. I thank you for your constant love for me. You seek me out and reach down into the fish's belly where I bury myself in excessive self-interest, workaholism, external-image making, and forgetfulness of those closest to me. The darkness of bad habits disguises my spiritual laziness and blinds me to the shower of graces you pour on me every day. Draw me out of spiritual darkness. During this Lent may I absorb the light of your truth and the warmth of your love.

Contemplatio

"[S]omething greater than Jonah is here!"

Thursday of the First Week of Lent

∴ ⋯⋯⋯⋯ ∴

Lectio

Matthew 7:7–12

Meditatio

> *"Ask and it will be given to you …"*

We have heard or read these words countless times—at Mass, on a retreat, reading Scripture. Their very familiarity could make them lose their impact unless we really think about them.

I once met a young woman who was not very religious. We were talking about the Bible, and I was amazed when she quoted this passage and told me that she tried to live her life by these words. She confided that she had been searching for meaning in her life and one day read this saying of Jesus. It struck her, and she found in it an answer to her yearning. She realized that God was the one she had been searching for, and that she could trust in God and his promises.

Jesus understands our needs, desires, and wants. How can we not be touched by Jesus' assurance that he hears us knocking and he sees us searching? This is not the only place in Scripture where Jesus makes this promise. For example, Jesus says in the Gospel of John, "whatever you ask in my name, I will do …" And he immediately repeats himself: "you ask anything of me in my name, I will do it"(Jn 14:13–14). And again, "If you remain in me and my words remain in you, ask for whatever you want and it will be done for you" (Jn 15:7); "whatever you ask the Father in my name he may give you" (Jn 15:16). He even says, sounding almost as if he is longing for us to ask for our heart's desire: "Until now you have not asked anything in my name; ask and you will receive, so that your joy may be complete" (Jn 16:24).

These words of Jesus strengthen our faith, making it a vital force in our lives. They are a true source of joy and hope, comfort and courage, inspiration and direction.

Oratio

Lord, help me always to place my faith and trust in you. Help me always to believe in your words and promises, confident that you will grant what I need for my spiritual good. Help me especially to remember your promise when I find myself overly anxious about my needs or the needs of those I love. Instead of fretting, I want to remember to turn to you and remind us both of what you have said: "it will be done for you."

Contemplatio

"Whatever you ask in my name, I will do."

Friday of the First Week of Lent

∴ ············ ∴

Lectio

Matthew 5:20–26

Meditatio

"You have heard ..."

This is the first of six brief passages in which Jesus "brings to fulfillment" the commandments given to Israel on Mount Sinai. He brings religion to the level of the Beatitudes, which he proclaims earlier in the same Sermon on the Mount. Jesus digs down to the roots of evil actions—in this case, to hostile thoughts and uncontrolled emotions.

Such thoughts and emotions can be dangerous to others as well as to ourselves, because they often lead to action—anger could lead to a verbal attack or violence. A time-honored saying expresses this: "Sow a thought and reap an act; sow an act and reap a habit; sow a habit and reap a destiny." Everything starts within.

Anger surges up when I perceive (or *think* I perceive) injustice. Therefore, not all anger is "wrong." What *is* wrong is *uncontrolled* anger. Saint Paul says, "Be angry but do not sin," and he adds, "do not let the sun set on your anger" (Eph 4:26). I need to cool off and, if possible, to be reconciled with the other party soon.

How to go about this is up to the Holy Spirit and me. Although Matthew's Gospel stresses morality, it doesn't give me a blueprint for handling difficult situations. My next move is left up to me in my concrete circumstances, acting under the guidance of the Holy Spirit.

I like to call Matthew the "Gospel of responsible freedom." Matthew calls me to the freedom of an adult child of God. The next time I get angry, I hope I'll ask God's help at once. (A quick SOS to the Lord could be a good replacement for the old practice of silently counting to ten.) I might also look for a harmless way of letting off steam. After I've cooled, I'll want to analyze the situation: Was there really injustice? If so, what are the options for addressing it? How and when will I try to seek reconciliation with the other person(s) involved?

Oratio

Lord, when I feel anger welling up, help me to be silent and pray for guidance. Enable me to look at the real or imagined injustice. If real, how—and when—can I address it? Guide me through those difficult moments. Help me to think clearly and channel my emotions appropriately. May I never forget that the person who has aroused my anger is my brother or sister. If he or she knows I was angry, give me the courage to ask forgiveness as soon as feasible.

Contemplatio

"But I say to you ..."

Saturday of the First Week of Lent

∴ ⋯⋯⋯ ∴

Lectio

Matthew 5:43–48

Meditatio

> *"So be perfect, just as your heavenly Father is perfect."*

This morning I happened to pick up a personal notebook that I had kept about fourteen years ago. I had written in it some resolutions about ways I could grow spiritually, noting several areas for improvement. Not much has changed in fourteen years! I had to laugh at myself because I realized that despite all my plans and good intentions, I still have to work on a lot of the same areas that I was working on back then. I'm pretty much the same person.

I suppose I could get discouraged at that. But it's probably the same for most people. We do grow, change, and mature through the years. But we also have our same personality, genetic makeup, and personal background that have stamped us in certain ways. I'll probably be writing the same resolutions for Lent until the end of my life.

And that's okay. God doesn't expect us to be perfect in the sense of not having any faults. He just expects us to keep on trying, to never give up the fight, and to keep on plodding along in our spiritual life. When Jesus tells us to "be perfect as our heavenly Father is perfect," he doesn't mean that we should have no flaws. The Greek word the Gospel uses for "perfect" (*teleiois*) has the sense of tending to grow to maturity. Something reaches perfection when it's fully developed, like a fruit tree bearing luscious, juicy peaches or plums. Jesus is not telling us to *be* perfect as if that meant a static state, to be achieved once and for all. Instead, he's telling us to always *strive* for spiritual growth. He's warning us against getting too comfortable in our spiritual lives. And if anyone can make us uncomfortable, our enemies can. Loving our enemies will surely move us along the way of perfection.

Oratio

Jesus, thank you for being so patient with me. Thank you for supporting me with your grace, even when I fall again and again into the same sins and failings that have been with me for years. Help me to climb out of the muck, wipe off the mud, and keep on going. I know that your hand will always be there to help me up. I ask for your grace to reach the goal you are calling me to and not to let myself get too comfortable along the way. I may have to stop and rest for a while, but I know that you will stay with me, Lord, and together we'll reach the goal.

Contemplatio

"Love your enemies and pray for those who persecute you."

Sunday of the Second Week of Lent — A

⠶ ·········· ⠆

Lectio

Matthew 17:1–9

Meditatio

> *"Lord, it is good that we are here.*
> *If you wish, I will make three tents ..."*

Take a moment and call to mind a time when you *knew* that God was present and at work in your life. Perhaps it was a moment of experiencing God's presence in the beauty of creation, or a profound moment of consolation during prayer, or a beautiful life event filled with the joy of Christ. These moments that are so permeated with God's presence are our mountaintop experiences. Like Peter, James, and John at the transfiguration, we too experience moments of profound grace and revelation in our lives—moments when we *know* God is in our midst in all his glory.

But, like Peter, we can be tempted to linger on the mountaintop. We don't want this moment of grace and consolation to end, and we are ready to set up camp! Although we can't stay on the mountaintop, I do think God wants us to bring this experience down the mountain with us. The transfiguration is set between two predictions of Christ's passion and death. This moment of profound grace is meant to prepare the disciples for the journey of the cross, giving them courage and strength for the sufferings they will soon endure. In fact, the transfiguration directly follows on Jesus' instructing his disciples that anyone who wants to be his disciple must "deny himself, take up his cross, and follow me" (Mt 16:24).

With its foreshadowing of Christ's future glory, the Transfiguration is not meant to nullify these words, but to give us the strength to live them, knowing that ultimately we are safe in Christ's hands. Peter wants to cling to this glimpse of Christ's glory and set up tents. Perhaps that is why the Father interrupts Peter's plans by reminding us all: "This is my beloved Son ... listen to him!" Jesus reminds us that he chose to come to earth not as King of Glory but as suffering servant. Jesus chose to embrace his own suffering and to walk with us in ours.

Oratio

Lord Jesus, what would it be like if I could truly recall the reality of your grace and presence in times of darkness and suffering? During this season of Lent, help me to remember your goodness at work in my life. As I call to mind your good gifts, fill me with gratitude and love for you, and may this love renew my strength. Then, when dark times come, help me to remember that you are with me, and that with you by my side, there is nothing to fear.

Contemplatio

"Rise, and do not be afraid."

Sunday of the Second Week of Lent — B

∴ ⋯⋯⋯⋯ ∴

Lectio

Mark 9:2–10

Meditatio

"Rabbi, it is good that we are here!"

Before the humiliation and loss of his crucifixion and death, Jesus gives three of his apostles an experience of his glory. Jesus knows of what we are made. He knows we are fitful and frightened creatures. He knows that we dread the cross, that we fear loss. So he brought these apostles to Mount Tabor to experience with him the glory that is his.

Our community receives prayer intentions from many people who entrust to us their most heartfelt desires or deepest fears and problems. We pray for these persons who are encountering the cross and bearing life's burdens. Though we all bear the cross in some way, in order to be like Jesus and to be with Jesus, we need to remember our own Mount Tabor moments. We all have had them.

These joyfully transfigured moments may have been celebrations of weddings, watching sunsets or sunrises with someone we love, the birth of a child, an experience of God's presence at prayer or the liturgy. If we can't remember a Mount Tabor experience, then perhaps our eyes have become more accustomed to the cross than to the transfiguration. Though the crucifixion and death of Jesus play an important part in redemption, they are only a part of the great paschal mystery, which includes the death, resurrection, and ascension of Jesus. John even refers to the death of Jesus as his glorification.

Even in the midst of the crosses we carry we need to keep our sight attuned to Jesus, who bursts in upon our lives with light, with hope, with the sudden surprise of resurrection.

It is hard to do this. Contradictions, failure, or fear can wear us down unless we are invincible in our courage. The best place to begin anew to expose ourselves to the transfiguration of Jesus is in prayer—not the prayer that pleads for what we think we absolutely must have, but the prayer that quietly asks for light and surrenders to hope.

Oratio

Jesus, now, today, in this moment, in this place I drop all thought, memories of the past, figuring out of the future. You want to meet me today. You want to shine in my life. Sometimes you immerse me in gentle light. Other times when I encounter you in your glory, it is like coming out of a tunnel into broad daylight. Today—how will you come to me? How will you transfigure my life? How will you prepare me for my share in your cross? Come, Jesus, come.

Contemplatio

How will you come to me today?

Sunday of the Second Week of Lent — C

:•   ·············   •:

Lectio

Luke 9:28–36

Meditatio

> *"... becoming fully awake, they saw his glory ..."*

O Lord, what will it take to wake me up? Why is it so hard to pay attention and to stay focused when I pray? Were we not meant to be united with you in deep communion? How easily I drift into sleep like your inattentive apostles! I can understand them; I try to work hard all day, to be present to people and responsibilities, to get things done quickly and well. And when I finally find some quiet moments to pray, weakness takes over so quickly. "Do as John did at the Last Supper and fall asleep on the Lord," a priest told me once in confession. I don't think he meant every time!

It is a consolation to know that you, too, grew tired and fell asleep during the storm at sea. As with your incarnation, in that incident at sea, were you giving us "permission" to be human? So often I try to carry more than I need to, and it doesn't work. It is impossible for me to do all I desire; no wonder I falter under the burden. "God is my co-pilot" the old bumper sticker proudly announced. "If God is your co-pilot," a more insightful sticker proclaims, "switch seats!" You are the Lord, not I.

But I want to stay awake! Not only in prayer, but in all of life. I want to live life deeply, fully present to those around me, my family, friends, coworkers, the person on the street. I want to keep aware of the sufferings of your people around the world. I want every person to know the dignity you have given them. But do not let me be tempted into making projects out of all this good; if I am present to you, I will be present to them. And when I forget you in my outreach to them, wake me up to your presence within them, and we will be reunited.

Oratio

Lord, you are the one who made us, and you made us with basic, built-in limitations like the need to eat, to drink, and to sleep. Our limited abilities and talents remind us daily of our poverty. What would be the outcome if we accepted these limitations as gifts from you to remind us of our total dependence on you? Like your great Apostle Paul, help me discover that in my weakness, your glory can shine forth (cf. 2 Cor 12:9). Help me become fully awake to your power and presence in my life.

Contemplatio

In my weakness, Lord, your power can shine forth.

Monday of the Second Week of Lent

∵ ⋯⋯⋯⋯ ∴

Lectio

Luke 6:36–38

Meditatio

"Be merciful . . ."

However it is translated, mercy or compassion is an essential, almost instinctive expression of all of the world's great religions. Jesus is not offering a ground-breaking revelation here, at least not with the first two words of his sermon! Most of today's Gospel passage simply develops this first, essential precept: Be merciful. The short passage from Luke may even seem to be just a long list of difficult moral commands—except that a promise is matched to every aspect of mercy: do not judge (and you will not be judged); do not condemn (and you will not be condemned); forgive (and you will be forgiven); give (and gifts will be given to you).

Jesus seems to be making a basic human observation. We can imprison ourselves in a world of judgment and condemnation when these are our typical ways of dealing with others (or with ourselves). In other words, we inhabit the world we ourselves create, whether it is a world of mercy or of judgment. And this is where the Gospel makes a unique contribution. Almost unnoticed, in the very first line, is the "measure" Jesus wants us to use: "as your Father." Theologians speak of the human person as *capax Dei*—capable of bearing God. Jesus wants us to be "super-sized" to God's own dimensions, and he spells out what that looks like.

It can be tempting to dismiss the whole idea as impossible, and it would be if the starting point were not God's already overflowing gifts of grace. It is when we recognize the signs of God's goodness and mercy in our daily life that we can "be imitators of God as beloved children," led day by day to "live in love, as Christ loved you" (cf. Eph 5:1–2).

Oratio

Sometimes, Lord, I just don't want to hear another word of your Gospel! It sounds so beautiful, but I tend to go at it as if it were simply a matter of will power, and I get discouraged pretty quickly when my strength or good will runs out. But by telling me to be merciful "as the Father" is merciful, you are hinting that the Father is not simply the pattern, but the *source* of mercy. This is not something I am expected to do on my own! You want to live in me, continuing your ministry of compassion, forgiveness, generosity. It all starts with you: with your overflowing mercy in my life. I want to be so amazed, glad, and grateful for what you have done for me that I let your mercy spread far and wide. Open my eyes today to your presence, your grace, your mercy.

Contemplatio

"Merciful and gracious is the Lord."

Tuesday of the Second Week of Lent

∴ · · · · · · · · · · · ∴

Lectio

Matthew 23:1–12

Meditatio

"They preach but they do not practice."

It's comfortable to say, "Oh, those Pharisees!" and move on, thinking that this passage isn't relevant today. But is that really true? Let's look at the Pharisees.

They were lay religious leaders who wanted to observe God's law so perfectly they had built up another body of laws to help them do so. They also wanted other people to follow the same rules. These rules were difficult, so some of the Pharisees prided themselves on their strict obedience. They acted superior to people who failed. Some seem to have become so bogged down in laws of human making that they placed these above the commandments of God.

Jesus was open to the Pharisees. He accepted their hospitality. He welcomed Nicodemus, who came to him as a sincere seeker of truth. But Jesus had a problem with the way some Pharisees lived. And Matthew reported this for the benefit of his Christian community.

In religious movements there's a danger that laws will multiply and people will become so bogged down in seeking perfection that they stifle the breath of inspiration. This may be why Matthew quoted Jesus' recommendation to give God's commandments more importance than an abundance of human precepts. He also quoted Jesus' directives to avoid titles and honors and to live in humble service.

It's an important reminder for anyone in leadership. As we're told elsewhere in the Gospel, much is expected of anyone to whom much has been given.

But this teaching doesn't stop with leaders. We're *all* called to live what we believe. Each of us can ask himself or herself: How many times in the past twenty-four hours have I given a bad example? How can I become a better follower of Jesus?

Oratio

Lord, forgive me. Often I think I'm quite good, and I can't understand why others don't do such good deeds as I do, or why they don't shun the vices I avoid. When I'm thinking this, you sometimes—mercifully—let me fall flat on my face. And then I see how imperfect I am. Thank you for such moments! Please continue to enlighten me each time I begin to stray. Help me to *really live* what I believe. Let me recognize everyone as a brother or sister to be respected, loved, and humbly served after your example.

Contemplatio

"The greatest among you must be your servant."

Wednesday of the Second Week of Lent

∴ ⋯⋯⋯⋯ ∴

Lectio

Matthew 20:17–28

Meditatio

"What do you wish?"

Throughout the Gospels Jesus knows what people are thinking or saying among themselves without having to ask them. Why then does he ask the mother of Zebedee's sons what she wants? Surely he already knows that she wishes honor for her sons.

I think Jesus asks her so that she can voice her desire. Then this becomes a way he can enter into conversation with her so as to guide her to a different way of thinking. The exchange begins by this simple woman telling Jesus what she wants for *her* children. She is not concerned about what will happen to Peter or Nathaniel—her concern revolves around what pertains to her. Jesus' response will help her to stretch her mind and heart.

The "all about me" attitude that is prevalent in our day and age is not new. Here it is played out among the disciples of Jesus. To this mother's request Jesus responds that he is guided by the will of the Father. Jesus always defers and looks to what the Father wants or wishes, and he invites us to do the same. As Jesus speaks to the twelve he points out that the will of God is not the "all about me" attitude; rather, it is the "all about the other and God" attitude.

God is always open to hear what we wish. We pray for loved ones, for our needs and theirs; we may even pray in thanksgiving. But prayer is a communication from us to God *and* from God to us. We are invited in this conversation to ask, "God, what do you wish me to do in this situation?" "Lord, what is *your* will for me today?" As Jesus points out, we are called to be servants. To discover how and in what capacity we are being specifically asked to serve we must ask, "What do you wish, Lord?"

Oratio

Master, you can read the desires and needs of my heart better than I can give voice to them. I trust in your greater wisdom knowing that your wish for me is fullness of life for both my brothers and sisters and myself. Therefore, I ask you to give me today what *you* wish—what you perceive to be my deepest need. Guide me in the choices of this day so that your wish, your will, be done in me and through me. Whatever you wish, Master, that is my wish today.

Contemplatio

"Not to be served but to serve."

Thursday of the Second Week of Lent

∴ ⋯⋯⋯⋯ ∴

Lectio

Luke 16:19–31

Meditatio

> *"If they will not listen to Moses and the prophets . . ."*

Jesus, I have heard this parable so many times that it may have lost its effect. Lazarus has become an icon of the plight of the poor. I see so many Lazaruses on television and on the streets. But deep down inside I too have become like the rich man, unmoved by their unspoken cry. Why?

Today, I heard your story proclaimed again. I was struck not by the rich man or Lazarus, but by the rich man's brothers. "I beg you, father," pleads the rich man, "send [Lazarus] to my . . . five brothers, so that he may warn them, lest they too come to this place of torment." Abraham responds that they have received the message of Moses and the prophets and should listen to it. Knowing that they have not listened, the rich man reasons with Abraham that they would listen to someone who came back from the dead. Wisely, Abraham answers, "If they will not listen to Moses and the prophets, neither will they be persuaded if someone should rise from the dead."

In my heart, I have at times smugly reasoned, *"I would listen if someone came back from the dead."* The reality is that someone *has* come back from the dead—you, Jesus—but have I listened if I too am numb before the many Lazaruses in my life? Am I like the rich man's brothers?

The root of the issue is selfishness, which is so embedded in human nature that not even Jesus' resurrection has moved us to uproot it. My own selfishness enters so automatically into what I say and how I act. Something deep within me directs me to seek my comfort, fulfill my desires—to satisfy myself. I put so much energy into my own pursuits that I often don't even notice or don't have the energy to respond to the Lazaruses around me.

Oratio

Jesus, you promised that your Holy Spirit would remind us of all that you have said. I beg you to send your Holy Spirit to remind me of your message and to open my heart to receiving and acting on it. May your rising from the dead touch my heart and heal me of my selfishness. During this season of Lent, help me to deny myself in little ways, and take up my cross so that I may follow you instead of myself.

Contemplatio

"Be compassionate as your heavenly Father is compassionate."

Friday of the Second Week of Lent

:• ··········· •:

Lectio

Matthew 21:31–43, 45–46

Meditatio

> *"The Kingdom of God will be …*
> *given to a people that will produce its fruit."*

What a tragic parable Jesus tells us in today's Gospel reading. This thinly veiled story describes the rejection and death of the Son. God did not allow his plan for the salvation of humanity to be thwarted, however. God's Kingdom will be given to a people that will produce the fruit that God desires.

Through our baptism we have become members of this people. How can we produce the fruit that God desires? We find the key in the Scripture passage that Jesus quotes: "the stone the builders rejected has become the cornerstone." Jesus is this cornerstone. Our lives and our very beings must be grounded in him. This began at our baptism when we became members of Christ and his Body. Now we seek to grow in him, becoming more like Jesus every day.

Practically speaking, how can we do this? We begin by trying to know Christ better, through conversation with him and through thoughtful reading of the Scriptures, especially the Gospels. As we become more aware of Jesus' teachings, we try to think as he does so that our beliefs, thoughts, and attitudes become similar to his.

Our days are filled with actions, words, and choices, and in them all we seek to imitate the virtues that Jesus practiced.

We fumble along, doing the best we can—and realize that we cannot resemble Christ by our own power alone. We need God's help and grace. Jesus obtained this grace for us with his death and resurrection. Therefore we seek to grow in grace, especially through daily prayer, participating at Mass, and receiving the Eucharist and the sacrament of Reconciliation. The more Jesus is the cornerstone of our lives, the more we bear the fruit God desires. Let us rejoice, for "by the Lord this has been done."

Oratio

What an immeasurable gift, Lord, to be one of those persons to whom the Kingdom of God has been entrusted! How I long to bear good fruit! I recognize that it is only possible through your assistance and grace. Please help me, Jesus. Fill me with your grace so that I will be grounded in you today. May my thoughts, attitudes, desires, and behavior resemble yours. When I become discouraged, enable me to trust more wholeheartedly in you. When I begin to rely on my personal resources alone, please assist me to turn to you. Please, Jesus, be the cornerstone of my life. Amen.

Contemplatio

Jesus is the cornerstone of my life.

Saturday of the Second Week of Lent

:• ·········· •:

Lectio

Luke 15:1–3, 11–32

Meditatio

> *"While he was still a long way off, his father caught sight of him, and was filled with compassion."*

Luke's parable of the prodigal son moves me every time I hear it. It is too close to home. Who among us has not known the comparison and competition that makes us look at one another as rivals rather than brothers and sisters? We fear there will not be enough (of whatever), and we'd better protect our share. Who will look out for Number 1, if I do not? Our loved ones look on in sorrow, but we take our share and off we go. The younger son wants his inheritance, and he wants it now.

Without question, the father grants his son's request, gives him his portion of the estate, and lets him go. He knows his son, knows he does not yet have the maturity, the experience, or the wisdom to make all the "right" choices. How vulnerable he will be in this cold and dangerous world! The son has to make his own mistakes, perhaps many of them. And they will hurt. With sorrow the father lets him go, but I believe also with generous love and with trust. Trust that the goodness hidden in the depths of his son's heart will win out, trust that God is at work in his son.

And the father's love is not disappointed! His trust in his son is at last proven true—the son comes to his senses and returns home. "While he was still a long way off, his father caught sight of him, and was filled with compassion." It seems the father was on the lookout for his son, certain that he would return, convinced that the love he had poured out on his son would yet bring him home. In fact, we have a Father who is never about keeping everything to himself—but one who deeply desires to share with us everything he has.

Oratio

Father, are you also at work in me and in the people I love? Have you placed such goodness in me that you are convinced that I can and will return home to your mercy? Even when I am a long way off? Are you always on the lookout for me, always ready to welcome me back, to restore to me the wealth of grace and dignity that I sometimes squander? Help me trust in your love within me and within everyone else on this journey of life. And let me trust that you have love enough for all of us.

Contemplatio

My heavenly Father knows what I need (cf. Mt 6:32).

Sunday of the Third Week of Lent — A

∴ ············ ∴

Lectio

John 4:5–42

Meditatio

>*"Jesus, tired from his journey, sat down there at the well."*

The woman was climbing the hill with a water jug in her usual blasé manner. It was midday—not an hour for the village gossips or anyone else to go trudging out to the well. She felt free and content—at least as much so as she ever did. But who was that man sitting on a boulder in the shade? No matter, she thought. He wouldn't have anything to do with *her*. He was probably a Galilean. She had met some on the path a few moments before. Of course, they had ignored her and she them. She arrived at the well and reached for the bucket.

But, how strange! This *Jewish man* was speaking to *her*, a *Samaritan woman!* She replied abruptly, but he continued to converse. Now he was speaking of giving her living water. Fresh, running water? Impossible! Where would he get it? This man was a dreamer for sure …

She grew more and more puzzled. Now he was speaking of *lasting* water that would never have to be replenished. How much easier life could be if she had that kind of water! Imagine! (But what, she wondered, did this man mean by "eternal life"?) "Go call your husband" he was saying now. She froze. Did he *know?* Yes he knew! He was saying that she had had *five!* He knew too much—this strange Galilean. But she sensed that he did not condemn her, neither in his voice nor in his eyes. They had a spark of challenge, perhaps, but he really seemed to accept her. Now she realized that he hadn't been talking down to her at all. Perhaps he was a prophet. She asked a question about worship, and his answer made her wonder if he could be the Messiah. Rather timidly now, her bluster gone, she dropped a hint.

Yes! He admitted it! This news was so great that she had to tell somebody—*everybody!* As she left her jug and hurried down the hill, she was marveling that this person knew everything she had ever done—but still accepted her.

Oratio

Lord, may I never forget that no matter how much I've bungled—no matter what a mess I've made of things—you still love and accept me. Moreover, you're with me to help me work things out. Increase my faith in you. Give me the grace to make a new start—to begin over and over again if necessary. And help me to make your tender acceptance, your genuine concern, known to my family and friends. Help me to bring *them* closer to you, too.

Contemplatio

"Come see a man who told me everything I have done."

Sunday of the Third Week of Lent — B

:· ··········· ·:

Lectio

John 2:13–25

Meditatio

> *"[S]top making my Father's house a marketplace."*

It is easy when we read Scripture to comment upon how Jesus interacted with others. Look at those people Jesus drove out of the Temple! Imagine challenging Jesus like that!

The treasure of Scripture, however, is that it is really about *us*, about how Jesus interacts with you and me. Jesus comes into our practice of religion and overturns what we think had been good. I arrive at church on time. I drop my kids off at CCD. I volunteer to count the money three times a year. I cantor at the 12:15 Mass. I've entered a religious community of women and spend my life taking care of the elderly.... We too can settle into routine, just as the people selling animals for sacrifice in the Temple had settled into a routine expression of their religion.

Routine is not all that bad. At first it remains connected to the deeper meaning and motivation that prompts a way of living or believing. But what is simply routine over time can become disconnected with the deeper values that permeate it and slip into a rut, gradually degenerating over time into a mindless, heartless activity we no longer know why we are carrying out. Completing the activities of religious practice can then hide a heart that does not belong entirely to God.

Zeal for his Father's house led Jesus to shake up the system, in a sense to force a personal answer to the questions: Why are you here? What are you doing? What do you expect of God? What have you given to God? What is your whole life all about? Jesus' words refer to a prophetic verse in Jeremiah: Do not come to the Temple and say, "the Temple of the Lord, the Temple of the Lord, the Temple of the Lord," as though that would cover over other areas of your life where you cheat and lie.... You're making the Temple a den of thieves (cf. Jer 7:1–11).

Ask Jesus to come in and overturn those parts of your life where you have slipped into a rut; ask him to fill you with a zealous fire that burns with love of God.

Oratio

If I had been there that day when you, Jesus, came in and overturned all of our tables, doing what we thought was a good thing, I would have been angry and confused. If you come into my life today and force me to look at issues that I have safely swept under the carpet, I will be angry and confused. But I need you to do that, Jesus. So come gently but firmly, and show me where you would like me to change and grow into a deeper relationship with you.

Contemplatio

Help me out of the rut I'm in.

Sunday of the Third Week of Lent — C

⁘ ············ ⁘

Lectio

Luke 13:1–9

Meditatio

"[D]o you think they were more guilty than everyone else ... ?"

Two millennia later, we are still caught up in the details of disaster stories, fascinated yet horrified. The mention here of a falling tower evokes powerful memories of recent terrorist attacks and other disasters. We hear disturbing echoes of Pilate's brutality in reports of genocide, inhumane treatment of detainees, and a host of other misuses of power. We know too much about hurricanes, roadside bombs, tsunamis, guns in schools....

Whether the result of human cruelty or sheer accident, the evidence of evil at work is seductive. It not only manipulates those who are directly caught in its web, perpetrators and victims alike, but it affects onlookers as well.

Jesus responded to the terrible events of his day with sober words, "do you think they were more guilty than everyone else who lived in Jerusalem? By no means! But I tell you, if you do not repent, you will all perish as they did!"

These words remind us to look into our own hearts before drawing conclusions about other people who find themselves overwhelmed by tragic events. The sad truth is that it's quite easy to point to people and circumstances outside of ourselves and say, "Oh how terrible!" while completely ignoring the incongruities of our life.

We may or may not be able to do anything about large-scale disasters. We definitely can do something about the weeds of injustice, intolerance, insensitivity, etc., that sprout in our hearts and minds and choke off acts of goodness and mercy.

Taken as a whole, today's Gospel reminds us to use our energies to bear good fruit, and not to remain paralyzed at others' misdeeds or misfortunes. We started Lent with a cross traced on our foreheads and the words "Repent and believe in the Gospel." Repent *and* believe. Repent *and* bear the fruits of belief in the Gospel.

Oratio

Lord, I often hear so much news about terrible accidents and disasters. Chances are this morning's headlines involve loss of life somewhere on the globe—perhaps even down the street from me. Jesus, help me to keep my focus. Teach me to see the world through your eyes, with your compassion. Give me an attentive spirit that seeks to root out the causes of evil in my own life so that I may bear fruits of patience, kindness, goodness, and peace.

Contemplatio

"Repent and believe in the Gospel."

Monday of the Third Week of Lent

:• ············ •:

Lectio

Luke 4:24–30

Meditatio

"[T]here were many lepers in Israel during the time of Elijah the prophet; yet not one of them was cleansed, but only Naaman the Syrian."

In today's Gospel we see Jesus rejected by the people of Nazareth, his hometown. Jesus comments, "no prophet is accepted in his own native place." In the section of the Gospel preceding this passage, Luke tells us that Jesus had begun his ministry in Galilee, and word about him spread rapidly. He returned to Nazareth and spoke in the synagogue, amazing his neighbors by his words. They found him too much for them, and sarcastically said, "Isn't this the son of Joseph?" They could have added, "We saw him grow up. We know his family and where he comes from. Where does he come off preaching to us?" They expected that if God were to speak to them, it would be in some extraordinary way. Jesus was just too ordinary.

Jesus reminded them about the story of Naaman the Syrian, who was cured of leprosy by the prophet Elisha. Naaman at first got angry at the prophet, who told him to wash in the Jordan. There was nothing special about that. Couldn't he have done that at home? But his servant reasoned with him, telling him that if the prophet had asked him to do something special, he would have done it. So why not do what he was asked, even if it seems too ordinary? Naaman let go of his preconceived idea, went down to the river to wash, and was cured.

Sometimes God shatters our expectations by working in ordinary ways, through ordinary people. But we can miss what God is doing if we always look for something extraordinary or expect him to act in spectacular ways. The sacraments use ordinary things: water, bread, wine, oil, words. They're so ordinary that we might take them for granted and receive them routinely. Lent is a good time to pause and meditate on what we are doing when we participate in the Eucharist, and to receive it with fresh eyes and new love.

Oratio

Jesus, help me to see and appreciate all the ways that you act in my life through ordinary people. Open my eyes to see if I have any preconceived ideas about what you can do. I don't want to miss the action of your grace because it all seems too ordinary. I don't want to be like the people of Nazareth who rejected you because they couldn't see beyond their own ideas about you. Instead, help me to be like Naaman, willing to let go of my own expectations so that you can act freely in my life.

Contemplatio

"[N]o prophet is accepted in his own native place."

Tuesday of the Third Week of Lent

⁘ ············ ⁙

Lectio

Matthew 18:21–35

Meditatio

> *"The servant fell down, did him homage, and said,*
> *'Be patient with me.'"*

Another translation renders this phrase with much more intensity, truer to the expression of what the slave must have felt: he threw himself at the king's feet and begged for mercy. We can easily understand what that must have been like. We have each experienced the desperate feelings brought on by a relationship problem we couldn't fix, bills we couldn't pay, an accusation we couldn't clear. We've each in some way, at some time, been trapped, hoping that someone would at least just give us a break.

When we hear this Gospel parable, we often focus on the unforgiving servant. But in Lent I think God wants us to focus on the king. Pay attention to what the king does! When the servant says, "Give me a chance. I'll pay you back," the king's heart melts. He is moved and erases the entire debt. Erases it! Lent is the time to wake up to what God has done for us in Jesus. We could not repair the damage to our relationship with God caused by our sinful insistence in following our own ways, so God repaired it himself. Jesus erased our debt, stood in our stead, did for us what we couldn't do for ourselves.

We need Lent because we so often forget what the King has done for us. It is so contrary to what we experience from our fellow humans that we can't even conceive of the incredible mercy that would lead someone to give his life in exchange for another's. Such an unfathomable love recedes into the background noise of daily life. Lent is a giant wake-up call. The phrase "You snooze you lose" is so appropriate for this liturgical season. If we keep pushing the snooze button, we will never hear the awesome message, "This is what I have done for you! I love you! I will protect and save you! I will be with you no matter what happens!"

Oratio

What would it be like, Lord, if I lived like I knew who I was? How can I go through day after day, forgetting the larger context of my life? I am so safe in your hands. You have proven to me that your love is reliable. When life becomes desperate again, which I know it will, help me remember that you are right there beside me, holding me, guiding me, protecting me, leading me onto some mysterious path of goodness and safety. For you are my Redeemer and my Lord.

Contemplatio

I am so safe in your hands.

Wednesday of the Third Week of Lent

∴ ⋯⋯⋯⋯ ∴

Lectio

Matthew 5:17–19

Meditatio

> *"Whoever obeys and teaches these commandments*
> *will be called greatest in the kingdom of heaven."*

I remember a teacher I had in the fourth grade who taught our religion class. I'm sure we learned about the Ten Commandments that year, and probably the Beatitudes, etc. But this teacher yelled at us often and even made insulting remarks to the whole class, especially to certain students. This teacher could have been said to be teaching us the commandments, but she certainly didn't practice what she preached. The witness of her life contradicted her words, and, unfortunately, her actions are what have stayed in my memory until now, not her class lessons. "Whoever obeys *and* teaches...."

In order to teach others, we must obey the commandments ourselves. Our way of life needs to be consistent with what we believe. That's why Jesus also says, "Whoever breaks one of the least of these commandments and teaches others to do so...." To give a bad example is to teach others to break the commandments, especially if the bad example is given to someone we have greater influence over.

The opposite difficulty can also be found. One could be among those who obey the commandments, living good lives, but fall short, perhaps out of fear, of taking an active part in sharing or passing on the teachings of Jesus.

Many of us are blessed to have had in our lives people who both obeyed and taught the commandments of God. Most of us first learned about Jesus from our mother or father. We can probably also think of many other people who were models and teachers to us throughout our lives— schoolteachers, pastors, relatives, neighbors, and friends. The faith is always *received* through the mediation of others—their teachings and example. And as we have received, so we are called to give.

Oratio

Jesus, sometimes I find myself in a situation where I could explain something about the Church or your teachings to my friends or coworkers who are not Catholic. Often I'm too timid to do it. Other times, I exempt myself from living according to your way of life, which I hold everyone else to. Help me to live more honestly. Make me your bold disciple *and* apostle.

Contemplatio

Jesus, you are the way I want to follow.

Thursday of the Third Week of Lent

∵ .... ∴

Lectio

Luke 11:14–23

Meditatio

> "... *if it is by the finger of God that [I] drive out demons,*
> *then the Kingdom of God has come upon you."*

Luke's Gospel recounts the delightful scene of the Visitation, when the Spirit enabled Elizabeth to recognize the coming of the Lord among his people. Here in the doorway of a simple Jewish home, the Good News is first proclaimed between two women! This moment of great joy stands in stark contrast to the response of the crowds in today's reading. Rather than recognizing that God is in their midst, some accuse Jesus of colluding with the devil, while others seek to test him as Satan once did in the desert. They have not recognized the moment of their visitation—the moment when God has come to dwell with them.

During this Lenten season, I think the Lord desires to remind us that "the Kingdom of God has come upon [us]"—it is not a distant reality, but is present here and now, even as we await the final fulfillment of this promise. Do we recognize the moments of our visitation, rejoicing in the presence of our Lord at work within us and around us throughout our day? Yet for us Christians, recognition is only the beginning! We are called to be people of the Kingdom, making the Kingdom present in our world today as we offer others Christ's healing presence and love.

In today's reading, Jesus makes it clear that we each must make a choice in this regard: "Whoever is not with me is against me, and whoever does not gather with me scatters." Faced with these two conflicting sides, we must choose whom we will follow. We cannot stay on the fence, for if we do not choose Christ, we will be counted against him. Still, it is consoling to realize that for those of us who do choose Christ, the victory is already at hand! If we give our lives to Jesus, he will overcome the "strong man," casting out the darkness in our hearts and setting us free to love and serve him.

Oratio

Dear Jesus, I choose you! I want to be all yours, and to spend my life gathering others to you through the witness of my life and love. Like the crowd in today's Gospel, I know that I have often failed to recognize your presence within me and around me. Help me to become always more aware of the many ways you are at work in each moment of my day so that I can better come to know your great love for me. As this understanding grows, allow my heart to resound with gratitude and love. Help me to bring this love to all those I meet.

Contemplatio

I choose Christ.

Friday of the Third Week Lent

∴ ·········· ∴

Lectio

Mark 12:28–34

Meditatio

> *"Which is the first of all the commandments?"*

Many people love the opportunity to speak with an important or famous person. We remember the day, what the occasion was, the details of the event, what the person said. We might even have a photo of it that we take out and show people.

The scribe in today's Gospel seems to have felt this way about meeting Jesus. He had heard of Jesus and must have been pleased to have the privilege of asking him a question. Unlike many others in the Gospel, this scribe is not trying to find something of which to accuse Jesus. The scribe might have been a little "star-struck," but he was genuinely interested in Jesus' response. Imagine how he fixed his attention on Jesus, waiting for his reply. What did he expect Jesus to say? Was he surprised at the answer? Did he have his own opinion before hearing that of Jesus?

Probably other rabbis had responded with the Shema ("Hear O Israel, the Lord our God is one...." Deut 6:4) when asked what the first commandment was. Devout Jews prayed this prayer every day because it contains a central teaching of their faith. We can imagine the scribe nodding his head as Jesus recites the familiar passage. But then, something unexpected happens: Jesus goes on and answers an unasked question. The second commandment? "You shall love your neighbor as yourself."

Impressed, the scribe confirms what Jesus has stated. Jesus' final words of approval must have pleased this scribe and touched him greatly: "You are not far from the kingdom of heaven." If we would enjoy such affirmation from a celebrity or public figure, how much more should we look forward to it from our Lord.

Oratio

Lord Jesus, you are the most significant person in my life. Your affirmation of me is so much more important than what anyone else says or thinks. When I come to you and genuinely want to know what you think I should do, you will certainly enlighten my mind and strengthen my will in regard to the situation. Help me always do your Father's will.

Contemplatio

Jesus, what do you think about _____ ?

Saturday of the Third Week of Lent

∵ ⋯⋯⋯⋯⋯ ∵

Lectio

Luke 18:9–14

Meditatio

> *". . . O God, be merciful to me a sinner."*

Jesus tells this story of the tax collector and Pharisee in order to contrast two types of "posture" before God. The first is the one taken by a certain Pharisee, who would have been considered holy by the religious standards of Jesus' day. The second is the one taken by a certain tax collector, who would have been outside of the Jewish community due to his profession. Their standing before God is completely the opposite.

The Pharisee literally "took up his position," assuming a posture of prayer proper to his religious standing. His exterior posture betrays his internal attitude toward God and others. Strangely, Jesus says that the Pharisee "spoke this prayer to himself." This phrase may mean that he prayed quietly to himself. But could it also mean that he was praying to himself and not to God? After all, the Pharisee is actually trying to convince himself of his own superiority, worthiness, and holiness. He includes the tax collector in his prayer as a reminder to himself that he is better on the "God" scale.

But the tax collector, with an implicit decree of condemnation hanging over him, assumes a humble posture: he "stood off at a distance and would not even raise his eyes to heaven but beat his breast and prayed...." He speaks his prayer to God, and does not tell God anything about himself but rather reminds himself, in a way, of how God had revealed himself over and over again—as merciful. Casting himself on this God of mercy, the tax collector allows no one but this merciful God to judge him. He allows God to be God and surrenders all judgment to him.

Thus, the tax collector, not the Pharisee, is truly in right relationship with God. God is his God in whose hands he places his current sinful situation, and on whom he waits for mercy and redemption.

Oratio

O God, I so want to belong to you totally, in my thoughts, words, and deeds, but I see my frailty, weakness, and sinfulness. Let me allow you to love me because I am weak, sinful, and poor, not because I am perfect. Help me to embrace my pain, humanity, and sorrow so that in your love they may become my joy, hope, and wealth. Let me appear as a child before you, my Father—helpless, yet knowing that you would never refuse me your love. Let me be yours forever, and you will always be mine. Amen.

Contemplatio

"For my thoughts are not your thoughts, nor are your ways my ways, says the LORD" (Isa 55:8).

Sunday of the Fourth Week of Lent — A

∴ · · · · · · · · · · · ∴

Lectio

John 9:1–41

Meditatio

> *"Neither he nor his parents sinned; it is so that*
> *the works of God might be made visible through him."*

When the no-longer-blind man's parents are asked about their son, they say, "We know ... that he was born blind." Those words reflect a lifetime of sorrow: the initial realization that their newborn son would never see; the pain of watching him grow up deprived of what all the other children had; the suffering of seeing this strong, healthy young man reduced to begging because he could not work to support himself. "Born blind." Did they ask themselves why? Did they assume it was due to some sin of theirs? Did they beg God for his healing?

Jesus explicitly states that suffering of this kind is not a punishment for sin. But his "explanation" of what that suffering *is* might also disturb us: "so that the works of God might be made visible through him."

His suffering would help us *see* the works of God. Yes, by the end of the story, we do see the works of God in the healing of the man's eyes. But for all those years of blindness, the man and his parents could not have known that light and sight were coming. While the man was still physically blind, his parents were also blind—blind to the mercy of God that would later be revealed.

Is this perhaps how it is with us sometimes, when we are suffering some kind of pain, difficulty, or crisis? At the time, it's hard to have faith and wait for the works of God to be made visible. Yes, in hindsight, we can see how God has worked through pain in the past, that good has come out of evil, that suffering has made us stronger and better people. But in the moment of suffering, we are blind to the works of God that will come to light—blind with a blindness that may not be lifted for many years, perhaps not even on this side of eternity.

Oratio

Jesus, this blind man didn't even ask you to heal his eyes. Never having seen before, he may never have hoped that he would see.

I have seen. I have experienced your power working in and through my darkness, weakness, and pain. Help me to remember to look at my difficulties with the eyes of faith. And for those who are suffering blindly right now, work in their darkness and bring light soon to each one, especially those who lack hope of any change or healing.

Contemplatio

With the eyes of faith, I can see.

Sunday of the Fourth Week of Lent — B

∴ ⋯⋯⋯⋯ ∴

Lectio

John 3:14–21

Meditatio

> *"God so loved the world that he gave his only Son ..."*

The liturgy proclaims that God sent his Son to redeem us. How hard it is to wrap our minds around this fact! The Creator of the universe loves human beings so much that his Son entered into and endured our human condition, gave his life for us, and will continue to be one of us for all eternity! Mind-boggling. If we start to think about this, the question comes spontaneously: *Why?*

The age-old answer is still valid. We humans hadn't gotten it right. We hadn't taken the natural law implanted in us seriously enough, or at least we were too weak to follow it well. We continued to hurt ourselves and others. Our attitude toward God was skewed. God was someone to fear when nature's forces were unleashed, or to try to manipulate when we wanted to have our way. God was not someone to love. Yet God had created human beings so that he might enjoy our company, love us, and be loved in return.

Only God could "break through our deafness," as Saint Augustine would say, and get our attention. Only he could restore the right relationship between him and us. His choice of *how* to do this was astounding. He became one of us and died for us. "No one has greater love than this" (Jn 15:13). If we let this sink in, the sensational in contemporary life becomes trivial—headlines, films, novels.... Can anything be more sensational than the love of God for the human race?

How can we better appreciate this love? How better know the mind and heart of such a God? Again, there are age-old answers: reading or hearing the Word; praying; trying to live uprightly. As today's Scripture passage says, "whoever lives the truth comes to the light." It's the challenge of a lifetime, and *now* is the best time to start. "Today is the first day of the rest of my life."

Oratio

Jesus, help me to understand the love that motivated the Father to send you into the world. It is the same love that compelled you to live and die for me. Show me the relative unimportance of so many other things in my life. Give me a new perspective. Help me to see that coming to know you and the Father is the challenge of a lifetime—a challenge I need to accept here and now, in this Lenten season. Enable me to live the truth, come to your light, and respond whole-heartedly to your love for me.

Contemplatio

[W]hoever lives the truth comes to the light.

Sunday of the Fourth Week of Lent — C

∵ ·········· ∴

Lectio

Luke 15:1–3, 11–39

Meditatio

"... his father caught sight of him, and was filled with compassion."

Jesus, this story reveals your Father's immense love for us. I picture the father in this tale standing on a hill, peering into the distance, his hands shading his eyes from the sun's glare as he searches for his lost one. One day he sees his bedraggled son. I hear the boy sob his sorrow and regret, "I'll be a hired hand." Instead, the father in his immense joy arranges an extravagant party. Locked in his father's embrace, the young man stammers, "Dad, you shouldn't. Can we be low-key about this?" As he dons his new clothes, he muses: "What a fool I've been. I thought I had finally achieved the *good life* in a far-off land. It took hunger pangs and a pigsty for me to see that in my father's house I had not only the good life, but the best life!"

My *distant country* is the space I cram with all that is not God. It keeps me far enough away that I, too, can forget— forget the Father's words in Isaiah, "you are precious in my eyes ... and I love you" (Isa 43:4). The distant country for others is the "good life" of money, ease, and success. A man recently confided to me, "My wife and I lived as if we did not need God. We were busy making money, getting ahead. Now everything is falling apart. I finally realized we need God."

The Father's love is like the unending cascade of water crashing over Niagara Falls. The falls' awesome power is but a hint of the eternal Father's passionate, thunderous outpouring of life-giving love. Its force pushes aside any excuse I can mutter for ever running away from his love. It catches us and throws us into the depths of his heart—a "heart on fire" for each person. Lord, I am sorry for the times I have gone away to a distant land and broken your fatherly heart.

Oratio

Jesus, my Master and lifelong Teacher, thank you for revealing the heart of your Father with this story. Thank you for the embrace of the Father's love and pardon that I find in the sacrament of Reconciliation. The world has many a prodigal son or daughter. Among them are some of the most despised people on this planet—terrorists, abortionists, pedophiles, perpetrators of modern slavery—all who need to return to you and experience the cleansing power of the Father's love. You died for them too, Lord, so I ask you to turn their hearts toward you. May they one day enjoy your love and forgiveness. Amen.

Contemplatio

"[W]e must celebrate and rejoice, because your brother was dead and has come to life again; he was lost and has been found."

Monday of the Fourth Week of Lent

∴ ………… ∴

Lectio

John 4:43–54

Meditatio

> " … *come down before my child dies."*

This story of the royal official takes us by surprise. It begins predictably enough: word has gotten around in Capernaum that Jesus is back—the one who turned water into wine at the wedding in Cana, saving the family name of the young couple and providing for the feast. As this Gospel story takes place, Jesus has already said some extraordinary things, but he hasn't yet performed any of the healing miracles described in the Gospel. We're about to see the second "sign" Jesus performs in the Gospel of John.

This royal official's son is seriously ill, to the point of death. He goes to Jesus and asks him to come and heal his son. Jesus challenges him, "Unless you people see signs and wonders, you will not believe." Here we have a father desperately concerned for his son, and yet Jesus is speaking of signs and wonders. The man loses no time. Ignoring what Jesus has said, with calm and measured insistence, the father demands, "Sir, come down before my child dies."

When our loving concern for another is so intense, so utterly anxious, we focus. All else is irrelevant—we zero in on our goal, determined to force a solution. Can anything distress a parent more than to see a child suffering? This father pleads with Jesus, who immediately relents. He gives the father everything he has asked and more, "You may go; your son will live."

Instantly the boy is healed, long-distance. In this case, it is Jesus who receives the wonder—a father's faith so profound it needs no explanation or proof. The requested visit from Jesus is unnecessary. The father goes directly home without another word.

Oratio

Do I dare be so direct with you, Lord? Perhaps too often I am not nearly so insistent, so determined, so convinced that you will reply. Lord, you responded immediately, completely, to that father's distraught plea. May my love for the needs of all your suffering people move me to be as direct and resolute with you in my prayer. Although you will not always answer the way I wish, I believe that in your goodness you are already providing for me, for my loved ones, and for all your people.

Contemplatio

"Lord, I believe. Increase my faith!"

Tuesday of Fourth Week of Lent

⁝ ··········· ⁝

Lectio

John 5:1–16

Meditatio

"Do you want to be well?"

Jesus asked the man waiting at the pool an important question: "Do you want to be well?" Although he did want to be well, the man admitted to Jesus that he needed help. Jesus then healed the man, commanding him to "rise, take up your mat, and walk."

As we ponder this man's experience, we reflect on our own inability to heal ourselves of our spiritual infirmities and sinfulness. We too are weak and incapable of overcoming them on our own. We need Jesus' help.

Lent is an opportunity for us to ponder more deeply the incredible truth that the Second Person of the Trinity became a human being specifically for this purpose. Jesus died and rose to save us from our sins and to sanctify us. This awareness leads us to turn to him in *our* need. When Jesus asks us, "Do you want to be well?" we cry out, "Yes, Lord, heal me!"

Through our experience we know that we will not be changed in a dramatic moment, but over the daily living of our life. God's grace and action free us from our sinfulness gradually. Little by little our thoughts, attitudes, desires, words, and actions become holier. As our love and commitment to God deepen, our need to try to do everything on our own lessens. This frees us so that we can more trustingly abandon ourselves to the care and action of God. Then he is able to more greatly effect our healing and transformation. Sometimes we will fall. But these become occasions for us to ask pardon, to renew our resolve, and to hear Jesus' words again: "Do you want to be well?" We repeat our response, "Yes, Lord, heal me," knowing that his healing words for us will be fulfilled.

Oratio

When I contemplate your healing of the man at the pool, Jesus, I pause to consider you as my healer. Sometimes I get so caught up in the busyness of my day that I lose sight of my desire to become a more spiritual person. Sometimes I even wonder if I will ever overcome my weaknesses. I recognize that by myself I cannot. You, Jesus, are my hope, my healer. You see my spiritual infirmities and sinfulness. With great confidence I turn to you and open myself to your loving and healing action. "Yes, Jesus, I want to be well. Please heal me."

Contemplatio

Jesus is my healer.

Wednesday of the Fourth Week of Lent

∴ ⋯⋯⋯⋯ ∴

Lectio

John 5:17–30

Meditatio

> *"... [W]hoever hears my word and believes
> in the one who sent me has eternal life...."*

Today we often live on overload. We're overloaded with a deluge of marketing messages and product choices. Some people have what has begun to be termed "e-mail attention deficit disorder." We live in anticipation of "the next"—the next gadget, the next president, the next film, the next sale, the next fashion—only to "downgrade" the next big thing within minutes of its arrival. For example, one magazine article noted that when the iPhone debuted, it took only thirty hours for the more than 270,000 people who had purchased it to switch from their current service contracts. Within only forty-five minutes of its debut, people's excitement began to wane and they began to expect the 2.0 version. These statistics seem crazy, but I've experienced the fever of the "next" in little ways in my own life. We are children of our culture. We can't escape the frenzy of "next." It makes us impatient with working our way through something like today's Gospel passage, which is long and complicated, demanding our focused attention. It would be so easy to skim through it on to something else, but in doing so we would make a mistake. In this Gospel passage, Jesus is stating that he is the Son of God. Rather than a boring lecture, Jesus is actually addressing what that means for you and me. As Son of God, as divine, Jesus continues his work of healing us. He raises us and gives us life; he will judge us at the end of time and give us eternal life. As Son of God, therefore, Jesus offers us treasures we won't find anywhere else. We don't have to wait for the next big thing. We can settle down and immerse ourselves in the eternal life we are given *now*. All he asks is that we listen to his words and believe, and he will bring us peace.

Oratio

Listen and believe. Jesus, my thoughts are in the future, and I believe things when I see them. How can I find peace by listening to the words of the Gospel again and again, believing in something I can't see now? There must be something better: some author who says it better ... some preacher ... some novena ... some visionary.... Like a butterfly I keep flitting from flower to flower, expecting to land on the spiritual jackpot. How silly I am. I already have everything I need. Help me calm my restless mind, shut my appointment book, close the e-mail, and pass over the ads. I promise to give you time, to listen, and to believe.

Contemplatio

"Jesus Christ, Son of God, I believe."

Thursday of the Fourth Week of Lent

∵ ⋯⋯⋯⋯ ∵

Lectio

John 5:31–47

Meditatio

> *". . . I say this so that you may be saved."*

Jesus is on trial. He has cured a sick man on the Sabbath, and has been accused of breaking the Sabbath rest. Appealing to his Father's activity on the Sabbath (such as giving new life) and saying that he simply does the same, Jesus has aroused his accusers to further wrath: he calls God his Father. In addition, they seem to think that Jesus' hint of equality with the Father means that he is setting himself up as God's rival.

In yesterday's Gospel passage, Jesus explains that he is God's obedient Son, who does only what the Father wishes. (Therefore, he is not the Father's rival.) In today's passage, since the Law requires that someone being tried have witnesses, Jesus accepts that condition. He wants to give his accusers every opportunity to believe in him and be saved. As witnesses, he appeals not only to the invisible Father but also to John the Baptist and to the life-giving miracles he himself has worked. Jesus also appeals to the Scriptures, declaring: "even they testify on my behalf." But, Jesus continues, his accusers resist the Scriptures and thereby refuse to *come to him to have life*.

Having made his defense, Jesus takes the offensive and declares that one day his accusers will be on trial. *Moses* will accuse *them* before the Father, "because he wrote about me," and "if you do not believe his writings, how will you believe my words?"

In reading this line, I think of that passage in Deuteronomy (18:15ff.) where Moses told the people that someday God would send them another prophet like himself, who would tell people everything that God wanted to make known. Christians have understood this to refer to Jesus.

We who have the grace of believing in Jesus accept God's Word. But do we treasure and cherish it? Do we try to plumb its depths? Lent can be a time to grow in our love for the Word, which brings us still closer to the Lord.

Oratio

Lord Jesus, divine Master, your Word contains abiding truths to guide us on the way to salvation. Many passages of the Old Testament, while complete in themselves, contain a further dimension that refers to you. And the New Testament revolves around your life, teachings, death, and resurrection. May I read and listen to your Word attentively, under the guidance of the Holy Spirit. May I try to penetrate it always more profoundly, that it may bring me ever closer to you, the source of eternal life.

Contemplatio

"... come to me to have life."

Friday of the Fourth Week of Lent

⠶ ⋯⋯⋯⋯ ⠶

Lectio

John 7:1–2, 10, 25–30

Meditatio

> *"You know me and also know where I am from."*

One of the first things that we ask people when we meet them is where they are from. Along with knowing a person's name, this information is an important part of getting to know others. This was just as important in Jesus' time as it is today.

In this Gospel passage from John, some of the residents of Jerusalem believed that they knew where Jesus was from. It is clear that Jesus' place of origin was connected with the claim some were making that he was the Christ, the Messiah, the "one who was to come" in the name of the Lord. But others, in order to deny that claim, used the fact that they knew where Jesus came from.

Jesus responded and "cried out," interrupting his teaching in the Temple. Whenever Jesus responds with such emotion, we need to be extremely attentive because of the depth of what he reveals through such emotion. "You know me and also know where I am from. Yet I did not come on my own, but the one who sent me, whom you do not know, is true." With this exclamation, Jesus corrected the mistaken "knowledge" of those who claimed to know where he was from. Unlike us, Jesus situated his origin, his point of departure, not in a place, but in a Person—the Person of his Father.

Knowing where someone is from is important because it helps us frame someone's identity. But if we do not know the Father, we will be unable to grasp Jesus' identity. We cannot put preconceived ideas or judgments drawn from such bits of knowledge as someone's place of birth onto Jesus. If we really want to know Jesus, we must free ourselves from this very human way of relating to others and allow him to reveal himself to us.

Oratio

I want to know you, O Lord. You told us that you came from your Father and that it was he who sent you to us. You also said that if we know you, we will know your Father also. Help me to let go of any ideas or concepts that I have about you that hinder me from truly knowing you. May I be able to distinguish your voice from other voices that do not faithfully communicate who you are. Open my eyes so that I may see you clearly; open my ears so that I may hear your words plainly; open my heart to receive you fully.

Contemplatio

"Whoever loves me will keep my word, and my Father will love him, and we will come to him and make our dwelling with him" (Jn 14:23).

Saturday of the Fourth Week of Lent

∴ ⋯⋯⋯⋯ ∴

Lectio

John 7:40–53

Meditatio

> *"Never before has anyone spoken like this one."*

Today's Gospel features two groups of people: those who critiqued Jesus from their own viewpoint, education, past experience, prejudice, or fear, and those who listened and tried to discover what Jesus was doing.

These are still the two possible ways of approaching Jesus. In fact, these are the two possible ways of approaching the Church, world events, family situations, and other people. Those who saw Jesus through their own lenses argued. They were divided because they could only see and hear what their personal viewpoint allowed them to see or hear. If they did not like someone's viewpoint, they honestly could not see or hear it. All the time they missed Jesus completely, never authentically encountering him.

Those who listened to him, such as the guards and Nicodemus, who earlier had come to talk to Jesus by night, *observed* Jesus. They stated how they felt; they didn't argue with the others. They were too much in awe to participate in petty, fragmented conversations.

In the third chapter of John's Gospel, Nicodemus learned that no matter how much he knew as a Pharisee, he had to start over, be born again, keep silence before an event that would reveal something to him that was larger and greater than his own thoughts and judgments.

This is a tremendous lesson for us in the Church today. We have to be wise and connect to sources where we can hear and see more than people's biases, agendas, or fears. We don't need to depend on the interpretation of the secular news for our information on the Church. We can log on to www. vatican.va and read Church news for ourselves. We can lose our time arguing with others about how we each see things, or we can spend our time nourishing ourselves reading the Bible or biographies of saints, or listening to spoken-word CDs about Scripture and spirituality. We can connect to the Lord directly in Eucharistic communion and adoration.

Oratio

It is difficult, Jesus, to measure the length and breadth of my worldview. All I know is that it is small and cannot contain the mystery of you or your Church, or any other person for that matter. Help me change from analysis paralysis to listening, observing, asking questions, wondering, and contemplating. Amen.

Contemplatio

Ask questions. Listen. Pray.

Sunday of the Fifth Week of Lent — A

⁘ ⋯⋯⋯⋯ ⁘

Lectio

John 11:1–45

Meditatio

> *"Now Jesus loved Martha and her sister and Lazarus."*

This Gospel gives us a precious bit of information about Jesus: he loved this family and counted Mary, Martha, and Lazarus as his good friends. Jesus stayed at their house whenever he was in town. They called him immediately when Lazarus got sick. Martha and Mary knew Jesus would want to know that the one whom he loved was sick. They must have hoped that he would come to be with Lazarus during this trying time. And because Jesus is who he is, they also surely hoped that Jesus would use his power to help Lazarus.

But they weren't just sending him a message because they had heard that he was performing miracles. Their action was not based on Jesus' reputation, but on their friendship with him. Jesus liked to visit them at their home and he enjoyed their company. He spoke frankly and familiarly with Martha, as when he told her not to worry so much about the details of hospitality (Lk 10), and here, when he speaks a little abruptly to her, as if to say, "What did I just tell you?"

We do not have to envy the friendship that Martha, Mary, and Lazarus enjoyed with Jesus, for this kind of intimate relationship with Jesus is ours, too. On the part of Jesus, it is a reality. He comes to stay with us every time we receive Holy Communion. He is interested in every bit of information about our lives that we care to share with him. He speaks frankly and openly with us if we are willing to listen. He comes with power and grace for healing whenever we need it. And if we doubt him or forget him in our busyness, his friendship doesn't grow cold or distant. He just smiles and reminds us, "Didn't I tell you … ?"

Oratio

Jesus, thank you for being my dear friend. Why do I sometimes act as if you don't care about me? Sometimes it feels as if you are far away, as if I have to send messages by courier, and I wonder whether they ever reach you. No, I know they *do* reach you and that you love me and plan to do whatever is best for me, even though, like your delayed trip to see Lazarus, it is not always apparent that what you do is best.

Contemplatio

Jesus, I trust in you.

Sunday of the Fifth Week of Lent — B

∴ ‥‥‥‥‥ ∴

Lectio

John 12:20–33

Meditatio

"I am troubled now."

How easily the promises of life turn to suffering! At some point life has betrayed all of us. In our youth we may have pictured life as a gradual succession of triumphs: health, education, employment, love, marriage, children, security, peace, etc. But then, almost imperceptibly, things change. Trouble comes. All the former contentment pales because we are troubled *now*.

This is what happens when a group of Greek pilgrims approaches asking to speak with Jesus. We know nothing about them other than that they desire this audience. In the *now* when we come upon them in the Gospel, they are seeking the satisfaction of meeting Jesus. John does not tell us if they ever got to speak directly with Jesus. They first approach Philip, who in turn approaches Andrew, and then the two of them approach Jesus. Did the Greeks accompany them, or did they have to stay behind to wait? We do not know, but the word from Jesus is about suffering. He says that suffering is near at hand for himself and that anyone wishing to follow him must be willing to die to all else.

Although he is speaking of fulfilling perfectly the plan for which he was sent, Jesus speaks of it as troubling. As a man he trembles at the prospect of the suffering to come. "Yet what should I say? 'Father, save me from this hour'?" Rather, "Father, glorify your name."

In the second reading, the author of Hebrews indicates that Jesus had to suffer his way to readiness with "prayers and supplications with loud cries and tears" (Heb 5:7). He learned from his suffering and was perfected by it, and only then was he able to become "the source of eternal salvation to all who obey him" (Heb 5:7–9).

The Greeks, who represent all of us, will have to learn the value of suffering. It is not that the Father glories in our suffering, but he glories in our readiness, our understanding, our desire to fulfill his holy will. And we remind ourselves that God's will *is* holy because it is his plan of eternal blessedness for us.

Oratio

Lord, may I learn from all the troubles of life, both those that are seemingly insurmountable and those that are only passing irritations, to prepare my heart for blessing. As my brother, you also had to learn the art of suffering. I unite with you as my Savior in suffering, knowing that our Father in heaven will honor those he finds in your company. Blessed be the troubles that lead me to the kingdom. Amen.

Contemplatio

Blessed be my troubles!

Sunday of the Fifth Week of Lent — C

∶• ⋯⋯⋯⋯ •∶

Lectio

John 8:1–11

Meditatio

> *"... he bent down and wrote on the ground."*

In all likelihood the poor woman caught in adultery was already humiliated by her sin, even before she was discovered. Now she is being paraded through the streets to the midst of a big crowd. "All the people" were there—including the scribes and Pharisees. Very quickly she realizes that she is being used by these men, too. They "made her stand in the middle," her life on the line, in a humiliating mock trial.

But it seems as though Jesus is being tried with her. All eyes are on the two of them, as people hurl the painful accusation at the woman. What does Jesus do? With the crowd's attention now riveted on him, he bends down and writes on the ground. What's this about? Scholars have speculated without conclusion about the significance of this action and what Jesus may have written in the sand.

Personally, I think Jesus' action was a simple gesture of compassion. When he got up, bent down, and began to move his finger in the sand, the eyes of all the people would have followed him. Their attention left the woman and went entirely to him. She must have welcomed this small distraction, to no longer be at the center of their accusing glare.

The scribes and Pharisees persist, however, demanding an answer. Jesus straightens up, telling them, "Let the one among you who is without sin be the first to throw a stone at her." And then, amazingly, he bends down again, and once more writes in the sand. He alone is that one without sin—and yet he occupies himself with the sand. Now, as the scribes, Pharisees, and others gathered there gradually recognize their own sin, they are not made to feel the same humiliation they had just forced on the woman. They can quietly slip away, unnoticed, because Jesus isn't even watching—he's playing in the sand. Only when Jesus is alone with the woman does he speak to her directly, "Neither do I condemn you."

Oratio

Lord, please teach me your compassion that I may offer courage to those burdened by their own sins. Help me never presume to judge another's heart, since I too have sinned. Help me be perceptive and creative in my love so that I may discover sensitive ways to help those who need mercy. May my help be respectful and discreet, so that others are able to claim their sin if they need to, but without fear, so they may also reclaim their dignity, with full confidence in your mercy.

Contemplatio

Lord, teach me your compassion.

Monday of the Fifth Week of Lent

∴ ⋯⋯⋯⋯⋯ ∴

Lectio

John 8:12–20 *(alternative reading)*

Meditatio

> *"Jesus spoke to them again, saying,*
> *'I am the light of the world. Whoever follows me*
> *will not walk in darkness, but will have the light of life.'"*

It happened on November 9, 1965. The Great Blackout left more than 30 million people in the Northeast and Canada in the dark. I was only nine years old, but I remember the night and the feeling of suddenly being plunged into the dark. At first it was exciting and even fun. But as the novelty wore off and we tried to make supper and do the dishes while stumbling around in the dark, we missed the light we had taken for granted. People were stuck in elevators, trapped in stalled subway trains, and caught in traffic jams. It turned out that a single faulty relay in one power station had failed. That started a cascade effect as overloaded electrical lines gave out, spreading through the power grid like falling dominoes.

As bad as all that was, though, it was nothing compared to spiritual darkness. How many people stumble today in the darkness of unbelief? Jesus called himself the light of the world, assuring us that if we have faith in him, he will lead us safely through life. At times we can take the gift of faith and baptism for granted. Jesus can become for us almost like the light switch on the wall that we never think about until a power failure hits. Lent offers us the chance to renew our relationship with Jesus. Even if we forget about him at times, he always stays with us. Through prayer, fasting, and almsgiving, our relationship with Jesus grows. Small things can have big effects, just as the faulty relay caused a major blackout. Four weeks of Lent have passed already. If our initial efforts have slackened a bit, these final two weeks offer a new chance to begin again. We will walk with Jesus along the road to his cross and resurrection. His grace will accompany us.

Oratio

Jesus, thank you for being the light of my life. May I never take you for granted, but live in a spirit of gratitude for the truth that you teach us, the truth that makes us free. Help me to treasure every word in the Gospel and meditate on it day and night. Your word is "a lamp for my feet, a light for my path" (Ps 119:105). Help me to listen to the words you speak in the silence of my heart.

Contemplatio

"I know where I came from and where I am going."

Tuesday of the Fifth Week of Lent

∵ ············ ∴

Lectio

John 8:21–30

Meditatio

"Because he spoke this way, many came to believe in him."

Many came to believe. People were attracted to Jesus, not only in Galilee but also in Samaria, Perea, and Judea—in this case in the outer courts of the Jerusalem Temple. Some of them declared they had never heard anyone speak as this man did.

But what became of those believers? We don't know the answer. I suspect that some were like the footpath and the rocky/thorny ground where the seed of the Word was snatched away, parched, or choked. After all, those were times of turmoil.

But I like to think that some of Jesus' listeners were "good soil." I can picture their joy when news of the resurrection began to be whispered from house to house. I see those people rallying around the apostles at Pentecost and joining the first followers of "the Way."

In any case, the evangelists tell us that there *were* people who believed in Jesus. By God's grace these Jewish monotheists opened themselves to the amazing truth that in this controversial teacher there was something more than human—something ... divine.

Not far in the future, the ranks of the believers would grow, set on fire by the apostles' courageous witness and bold proclamation. The faith of those believers would be confirmed by the silent witness of the empty tomb, and later by the dramatic witness of martyrs. From city to city the news was to spread, until throughout the Roman Empire people of Jewish and Gentile origin would be joining together in prayer to Jesus "as to a god," as Pliny the Younger, a Roman governor, would write in amazement.[*] Such was the transformation that the Holy Spirit was to bring about in minds and hearts.

Oratio

Lord Jesus, may I be good soil for the seed of your Word. May I ponder the Scriptures that tell about you and come to a deeper appreciation of your divine identity. The first Christians' belief in your divinity must have been somewhat unclear, though firm. Instead, I enjoy the fruit of Christian thought developed for centuries under the guidance of the Holy Spirit. Jesus, deepen my wonder and awe at the great mystery of Father, Son, and Holy Spirit—one God, living and true—a God who loves me and offers me everlasting happiness.

Contemplatio

"[T]he one who sent me is true."

[*] *Letter to Trajan* in English found at www.ccat.sas.upenn.edu/jod/texts/pliny.html.

Wednesday of the Fifth Week of Lent

:• ·········· •:

Lectio

John 8:31–42

Meditatio

"… no room among you."

During Advent we read in the Gospel of Luke about another case of "no room." Mary and Joseph were searching for a place in Bethlehem, a place where Mary could give birth to Jesus. Obviously, that case concerned seeking physical space for this small family.

Here Jesus speaks of "room" in our hearts, about our being open to the "tiny whispering sound" (I Kings 19:12) of God's voice in us and addressed to us. We are to listen not just with ears but also with an open and discerning heart, that we might be able to hear his invitations daily and act on them. God eagerly desires that these whispers be understood and acted upon so that God may dwell in us.

As I pray, I find myself gently probed to discover who else finds no room in my heart and in my actions. If we were to give Jesus as Word of God incarnate the room to dwell in us with all his energizing power, we would find room for every person who seeks it. We may not always be able to give in a way that would alleviate a physical need, but we can always give a person a home in our heart. We can always treat every person we meet with respect as a brother or sister.

Although the human family comprises a vast number of people, we are not so different in our needs. We each need to be loved and valued for who we are, not who we could or should be. We each need to be respected; we each desire to be seen and understood. Whether it's a homeless person, a coworker, a family member, or someone in the headlines, I can love and respect each person by the way I hold them in my heart. I believe that God dwelling in me wishes to make room for everyone.

Oratio

God of love and compassion, may your Word dwell in me and guide me to hear your whispers this day. Help me to really see the people around me, to hear their stories, to make time for them despite the busyness of my day and my preoccupations. Enlarge my capacity to love that I might give them room in my heart, for in giving them room I also give you more room. Love in me, live in me, breathe in me, and act in me. May others see you in me, and may I see you in others.

Contemplatio

"You are my friends if you do what I command you" (Jn 15:14).

Thursday of the Fifth Week of Lent

∴ ·········· ∴

Lectio

John 8:51–59

Meditatio

> *"If I glorify myself, my glory is worth nothing;*
> *but it is my Father who glorifies me...."*

This is Jesus' response to the challenge, "Who do you make yourself out to be?" His questioners think Jesus is getting above himself, putting on airs. They think he should be more humble and not make these wild claims to greatness.

But what is humility, actually? We may think it simply means not bragging about our accomplishments and gifts, or maybe even downplaying them. No, humility is truth, as many spiritual writers have said.

So if I *am* talented at something, I can go around saying it as much as I want, as long as it's the truth? No, that's not the kind of truth that is meant. It's a deeper truth. The deeper truth says that my talent is a gift. It does not come from me (even though I may have contributed my part by hard work and effort to perfect the gift). The deeper truth is that I have nothing of my own—every ability and capacity I have comes from God. All my bodily graces also are from God. So my good looks, my good deeds, and my good fortune are all given to me by God. My very existence is a gift—my heavenly Father loved me into being. So yes, it is our Father who glorifies us. Everything we have to glory in comes from him.

And my greatest glory? My greatest claim to fame? Jesus Christ loves me and gave himself for me. If we truly glory in this tremendous gift, then all else falls into place. The other bragging points (or lack thereof!) are put into perspective. The true reason for my great worth is not my attractiveness or my competency, much less the things I own or the positions of responsibility I have. The reason I am of infinite value, more precious than gold, is the value placed on me by my Creator and Redeemer.

Oratio

Jesus, I wish I could get this straight once and for all. I seem to vacillate between being proud of myself for the wrong reasons (my accomplishments, other people's good opinion of me, etc.) to being down on myself for the wrong reasons (my failures, other people's bad opinion of me, etc.). Help me to see and live in the truth of your eternal and absolute love for me that bestows on me, as a gift, all that I have and am.

Contemplatio

I glory in my Lord's love for me.

Friday of the Fifth Week of Lent

∴ ············ ∴

Lectio

John 10:31–42

Meditatio

"[M]any there began to believe in him."

Today's Gospel begins to prepare us for the momentous events of Good Friday, one week from today. It describes what happened when some people picked up rocks to stone Jesus. He pointed out that he had shown them many good works from his Father and asked, "For which of these are you trying to stone me?" They answered that it was because "you, a man, are making yourself God." Although they had seen the signs he worked, they did not believe. The people whom John describes at the end of today's reading, instead, "began to believe in him." What a contrast: unbelief and belief!

We have received the gift of faith, through which we believe all that God has revealed. How does our faith affect our daily living? For example, we know that Jesus redeemed us. Does our belief lead us to confidently ask for forgiveness whenever we sin? Does our belief that God loves us unconditionally enkindle our trust in his provident care for us and for those we love?

Faith grows with use—and life presents us with many opportunities. When we wrestle with greater or lesser questions, suffering, or darkness, it is time to delve deeply into our faith, sometimes struggling to believe. We may even be tempted to stop praying, but this is precisely when we need to continue.

In our Gospel today, Jesus tries to reason with those who want to stone him, to help them recognize the truth: to have faith. He is willing to do the same for us. Let us go to Jesus, asking him for the answers we need and for his help. He will not disappoint us. Although it may seem that solutions elude us, we will gradually recognize his hand at work. We will receive grace, strength, and eventually understanding. Little by little, our life will become ever more deeply founded on faith. Let us pray, "Lord, I believe. Help my unbelief."

Oratio

As I reflect on today's Gospel, Lord, I realize how shaky my faith sometimes is, yet I want to believe deeply. Perhaps part of the reason is that I don't think about the truths that you have revealed until something goes wrong. It is true that I can zip—and sometimes drag—through life without a thought as to why I am living. I don't even recognize your hand in my day. Lord, I do believe, but please help my unbelief. Increase my faith. Help me to believe more deeply and to live out of my beliefs today. Amen.

Contemplatio

Today I am called to believe.

Saturday of the Fifth Week of Lent

:• ·········· •:

Lectio

John 11:45–56

Meditatio

> *"Jesus no longer walked about in public. . . ."*

Only John's Gospel tells us about the relocation of Jesus and his disciples to Ephraim. This village was near the desert—and the desert is a traditional place for men and women to encounter their God. Surely Jesus wanted to spend time in communion with his Father.

I wonder what passed between Jesus and his close followers during those desert days. Some of the disciples, at least, knew that Jesus was in danger. Before Jesus set out to raise Lazarus from the dead, Thomas had heroically said, "Let us go to die with him" (Jn 11:16). I picture Jesus trying to spare his disciples the turmoil he himself was experiencing. There would be time enough for them to suffer something of what he was going through. They would soon witness his agony, taste the sorrow of separation, and fear that they themselves might be put to death.

It seems to me that at this moment Jesus was like a loving parent. Not long ago, a father and his three teenagers were lost in a forest during a raging five-day snow storm. The father was afraid they would never be rescued. But during their ordeal he concealed his fear for the sake of his children, who were likewise afraid. I can picture Jesus keeping a calm exterior in the presence of his disciples while his emotions oscillated between a clammy dread and an ardent desire to plunge into his passion.

Probably Jesus went apart from his followers often in those desert days. With his Father, he could be himself—disclosing the emotions seething within him and receiving comfort. No one else could have really understood.

It's consoling to think that whatever any of us has to endure, Jesus has been there. And he can be there for us. He's ready to share our every sorrow.

Oratio

Jesus, you understand! You know the anxieties and fears that we, our family members, and friends struggle with. The frustration of someone unable to find employment. The anxieties of spouses who can't seem to make their marriage work. The terror of someone facing terminal illness. When frustrated, anxious, or terrified, I might need to hide my feelings from those around me, but I can always turn to you, knowing that you understand completely. Jesus, meet me in my own inner desert. Help me turn to your Father for strength, as you yourself must have done in those lonely days at Ephraim.

Contemplatio

" . . . he left for the region near the desert."

Passion Sunday — A

∵ ⋯⋯⋯ ∵

Lectio

Matthew 21:1–11; 26:14–27:66

Meditatio

"Hosanna to the Son of David!"

What a heady beginning to the Passover festivities this day seemed to be for the apostles. It started out with this unexpected triumphant moment, when all their secret ambitions of glory and fame seemed to be coming true. Jesus rode into Jerusalem amidst the acclamation and praise of the people, the crowds going wild. Though the apostles had listened to the teaching of the Master about humility and the last place, the roots of ambitious excitement die hard. In fact, just listening to Jesus' teaching wasn't enough. Their ambitions would only die with his own death, when they would be hiding together in a dark closet somewhere, hoping to escape with their lives.

These two readings show us the span of a disciple's life. The exciting moments of conversion or successful ministry or busy activity must lead us into at some point to a transformation that involves death. Jesus' death on the cross meant the death of the apostles' ambitions, as it will mean the death of our own. Something happens that turns the tables. Illness, financial disaster, ministerial failure, disappointment, complaints about our work…. In a moment the popularity of Palm Sunday evaporates, and the frightening darkness of the agony in the garden and the cloudy confusion of Golgotha creep in. In the process we find ourselves playing the parts of each of the main disciples mentioned in the reading: the one who turns traitor, the confident boaster who eventually denies Jesus, the apostles who disengage themselves from reality, the brave young disciple who accompanies Mary to the foot of the cross. One by one, in event after event of our lives, we try these disciples on for size, each time discovering new facets of our own following of the Master.

In the journey we fall and are forgiven, fall again and are forgiven again. In the journey we discover that the cross does not have the last word, and never will. We are not people of the cross, but people of the resurrection!

Oratio

Jesus, in this moment of profound quiet, I ask you to come close to me, to look into my eyes, and to help me understand that no matter what has happened in my life, no matter who I've been in my life, I can keep on journeying with you as disciple and friend. Can you accept me in my lowest moments, when your cross weighs too heavy upon me? As ambition dies in my heart, let me learn I am loved. That's all I need.

Contemplatio

Let me learn I am loved. That's all I need.

Passion Sunday — B

⁝ ·········· ⁝

Lectio

Luke 22:14–23:56

Meditatio

"This is my body.... This cup is the new covenant in my blood...."

An interesting contemplative exercise would be to jot down in two separate columns the words said by Jesus and those said by everyone else in this Gospel passage.

The disciples and religious and civil leaders say things such as: "Who is the greatest?" "Lord, I am ready to go to death for you!" "Look, here are two swords. Shall we use them?" "If you are the Messiah, tell us." "This man perverted our nation." "Crucify him!" (cf. Lk 22:24–23:21).

Jesus says, "This is my body.... This is my blood, which will be shed for you." "The leader is the one who serves. I am among you as the one who serves." "You, Peter, will deny me." "Pray not to enter into temptation." "Judas, do you betray me with a kiss?" "If I tell you who I am you will not believe me." "Father, forgive them" (cf. Lk 22:23–23:34).

The words of the disciples and leaders are characterized by self-protection. They are the words of people seeking to plan and control their lives from within their own framework or perspective. They are words of violence toward others.

Their words reveal their desire to forfeit their identity for the safety of the rush of the mob. Jesus' words, on the other hand, show that he has made himself vulnerable, that he will hand himself over for the sake of others. Jesus wasn't trapped in his own fear of death, but knew himself to exist within a reality more spacious than his own fearful neediness, something ultimately good in which his life was held, beloved, even were he to die on the cross.

In a word, perhaps that was just it. The attitude of the disciples and leaders in the face of threat was one of non-acceptance and fear. Jesus' attitude was one of acceptance despite his fear.

Oratio

Jesus, when my plans, security, or future are threatened by the cross, I want to protect myself, like the disciples. I want to be first, successful, important, beautiful, happy. I think that if I plan things just right, everything will lead to success. I hold on to everything so tightly, and in grabbing things I crush them. It was only after your crucifixion and resurrection, when you forgave the apostles, that they realized that something greater was planned for their good, that the cross was not a threat and couldn't ultimately destroy them. They were beloved and safe. They discovered that they could trust you. And so can I. And so will I.

Contemplatio

I am beloved and safe.

Passion Sunday — C

∴ ·········· ∴

Lectio

Luke 22:14–23:56

Meditatio

"Father, forgive them. . . ."

The events of the passion are so many and so oppressive that they almost smother us. In reading this account from Luke, I find it helpful to focus on Jesus himself, rather than on what is being done to him. What does Jesus do and say? What thoughts and attitudes does he seem to have?

Throughout his Gospel, Luke focuses on the Lord's compassion. He continues to do so in his account of Jesus' sufferings and death. The Savior meets the women of Jerusalem and tells them not to weep for him, but for themselves and for their children. He promises the good thief that on that very day they will be in paradise together.

Of his executioners, Jesus says, "they know not what they do." We know that the executioners were only following orders. But were the men who *gave* the orders also ignorant of what they were doing? That wouldn't surprise me. Motives don't have to be totally evil to generate injustice. All too often in this world someone will act from self-interest, or for the benefit of a particular group, and cause other people to suffer because their needs and rights have not been taken into consideration.

People who wage war in the name of religion, or in the name of atheism, or even in the name of justice—don't most of these "crusaders" think their motives are good, even though their actions wreak havoc? On this Passion Sunday that cry rings in my ears: "[T]hey know not what they do."

Every Good Friday, the Church prays special petitions for all the people in the world. This year, I want to join in that prayer with special fervor, asking that the light and love of Jesus may reach far and wide.

Oratio

Jesus, heighten my awareness of the many people who don't know the purpose of life and the reality of the redemption. Inspire me to pray often that your grace may penetrate hearts. May everyone lost in darkness come to the light of your love. Give me a tender heart like yours—a heart of compassion for the whole human family. I want to pray frequently that your light and love may reach everyone, especially those who consider life meaningless and are trapped in hatred or despair.

Contemplatio

"[T]hey know not what they do."

Monday of Holy Week

∵ ·········· ∵

Lectio

John 12:1–11

Meditatio

". . . you do not always have me."

How often do these words occur to us as we try to pray? We are kneeling in church or sitting quietly, ready for prayer, but nothing happens. "[Y]ou do not always have me."

We may desire to pray, but feel stagnant. We might be engulfed in total silence; nothing stirs. The heart seems dead, the desire indifferent; and the mind faces a blank wall. Here we can thank God for the example of Mary of Bethany. Through her, Jesus illustrates the two ways of devotion found in the Great Commandment: besides prayer, which is service of God, there is service of neighbor. Jesus said to do both equally well with the whole mind, will, heart, and strength.

At first glance it would seem that the hero of the story should be Judas, who counseled prudence in the use of the valuable perfume. But Jesus reprimanded Judas, not for his suggestion, but because he was a hypocrite who himself was taking what belonged to the poor. So Jesus is not telling Judas to forget the needs of the poor and to squander valuable goods. Jesus is foretelling his imminent departure—preparing his friends to continue serving him in the poor and to do it as sincerely and selflessly as Mary was serving him, washing his feet and drying them with her hair.

Today's reading from John suggests that our Lord knows that we will have more opportunity to serve others than we will have to pray. He also understands that we will often be disappointed in prayer. He will not always seem present to us, but our brothers and sisters are always with us. In understanding this, we are blessed by the example of Mother Teresa of Calcutta. Her personal letters reveal that this is exactly how things were for her. She did not always feel Jesus present in her prayer, but she found him present in the needy. Jesus asks us also to squander our attention on him in the poor. Such generosity will enrich our prayer.

Oratio

Lord, you assure us that we will always have the poor with us because we ourselves are poor. We are often poor in the things of the spirit. We struggle to be virtuous and we struggle to pray. Consolations in prayer are few and far between, while distractions and weariness are common companions of our prayer. Teach us to fill up our spirit by emptying ourselves of all that does not serve you. Amen.

Contemplatio

The house of my prayer is filled with the fragrance of my care for the needs of others.

Tuesday of Holy Week

∵ ⋯⋯⋯⋯ ∵

Lectio

John 13:21–33, 36–38

Meditatio

"Jesus was deeply troubled."

Jesus, when I ponder this Gospel I feel sad at seeing you troubled. You had said, "Do not let your hearts be troubled." Now you are troubled. Ecclesiastes tells us there is a "time for everything," including "a time to weep" (Eccl 3:1–4). Now it's your time to be overwhelmed with sadness. Even in our emotions you chose to be like us in all things but sin (cf. Heb 4:15). At times I feel storms of sadness and troubled emotions. You did not shield yourself from the stabbing pain of a friend's betrayal. You wept over Lazarus and over Jerusalem. Your heart was moved with pity at seeing the widow of Nain. You knew the joy of friendship at Matthew's house and the comfort of the hospitality of Martha and Mary.

Now, Lord, you are plunged into a troubling sadness. You speak of betrayal and everyone acts surprised, even your betrayer. You tell Judas, "Do it quickly." Your sadness at Judas reminds me of what the martyr Saint Thomas More expressed in the play *A Man for All Seasons.* When Sir Richard Rich perjures himself as he falsely accuses More, the saint tells him that he is more troubled by Rich's perjury than by his own prospect of execution. What troubles you, my Lord, in this Gospel scene? The thought of impending betrayals and abandonment is breaking your heart. You know Judas' treachery. You look at the other disciples who seem so innocent and unaware of what will soon take place. You cannot force your love on the betrayer, but you try to save him. You wash his feet, you offer him the morsel dipped in the dish. Judas eats it and leaves. "And it was night." Judas walks out of your presence. He turns his back on the Light. He is swallowed by the night, by Satan, the prince of darkness

Oratio

Lord, Saint John details for us the love you offered to each disciple—even the one who would betray you. I ask you to be my motivation and my driving force, even when I feel drawn to abandon the cross of daily fidelity. May I care for those around me and desire their eternal salvation above all. May my love for others mirror yours—so I care for both their spiritual and their physical well-being. I trust that in your goodness you will grant me these graces. Amen.

Contemplatio

"My children, I will be with you only a little while longer."

Wednesday of Holy Week

⁚ ············ ⁚

Lectio

Matthew 26:14–25

Meditatio

"My appointed time draws near."

Throughout the Gospels, Jesus shows us that fidelity to one's vocation is lived one minute at a time. Jesus' fidelity is a lived out in a continuous stream of "now" moments: announcing the Kingdom of God, healing the sick, forgiving the sinful, all leading up to the appointed hour.

The Passover is beginning. Pilgrims are streaming into Jerusalem, including Jesus and his closest disciples. Jesus knows what is coming. "My appointed time draws near." Already in chapter 26 of Matthew he has foretold his crucifixion during the Passover (v. 2). He has declared the anointing at Bethany a preparation for his burial (v. 12). He knows, too, that one of his own disciples will betray him—an inside job.

In the face of betrayal, torture, and death, what does Jesus do? He goes on with his vocation of revealing the faithful love of God for his people. At this precise moment it means preparing and celebrating the Passover meal.

Betrayal is devastating. It is hard to say what is worse, to be caught off guard or to see it coming. Either way the sin of betrayal kicks us in the gut when we experience it. The example of Jesus is all the more astounding because, while he acknowledges Judas' betrayal as it is happening, he does not change his plans to avoid the situation. Neither does he lash out at Judas or retaliate in any way. Jesus, the absolute expression of God's love, is not sidetracked. Instead, he continues to freely give of himself.

Today we stand on the brink of the Sacred Triduum, and the Church gives us the calm deliberate choices of Jesus to continue his mission. He knows this will lead to Calvary. We also ponder the calculated moves of Judas, which will lead to his duplicitous kiss.

Fidelity (or its opposite) is lived out moment by moment, choice by choice. What is God calling me to in *this* "hour" of my salvation?

Oratio

My God, I want to be with you completely in these days when we remember your passion and death. When I think of your fidelity to your vocation, your total self-giving in the face of the betrayal and the cowardice of your disciples, I am overwhelmed. Time is a precious gift; help me to spend it wisely as you did in your public ministry. Strengthen me so that in my moments of crisis I may choose faithful love no matter the cost.

Contemplatio

Faithful love is lived out moment by moment.

The events of the Paschal Mystery,
the suffering, death, and resurrection of Jesus,
together comprise the pivotal point of time.

Everything that came before
and all that follows after
are defined by this, are transformed.

Holy Thursday

⠶ ··········· ⠖

Lectio

John 13:1–5

Meditatio

> *"[Jesus] began to wash his disciples' feet."*

For three years these twelve followers of Jesus had listened to him preach, watched him heal and raise the dead, felt his power as he forgave sins. But now Jesus was doing something unexpected. Evening meals had been times of camaraderie and conversation, discussion and sharing. Tonight, however, Jesus was coming uncomfortably close. The conversation died down as Jesus knelt and tenderly washed and dried their feet. In this act, at this moment, Jesus seemed to say, "Everything that has gone before has been a preparation for this. Knowledge, information, and moral conversion are not enough." He broke through all their inner barriers with this act of gently washing their feet. And he got their attention!

Imagine washing the feet of family members, friends, employees, employers, or enemies. It is an uncomfortable thought because it is so physical and so intimate. We often treat each other like shoe salesclerks. We'll help others fit their shoes, but we'll rub our noses as we do so, sit as far away as we can, and stay with them only as long as necessary.

(And please keep your socks on.) Instead, Jesus is calling us to relate to one another as hospice nurses washing a terminally ill patient. What tenderness, gentleness, and acceptance there is on the part of nurse and patient in this act of vulnerability!

As Jesus knelt before his chosen apostles, he said that with this act of physical contact: "I know you. I know all about you, and I love you. I will keep on loving you." It is difficult to believe that Jesus can know us *and* love us. It is even more difficult for us to know another and love that person.

Perhaps that is why Jesus continues to sustain this prolonged personal contact in the Eucharist. As the Last Supper, the Eucharistic Celebration is about familial, human, essential things, where we too are touched, held, and washed by Jesus in very intimate ways.

Oratio

Jesus, wash from me the leprosy of self-hate. Wash me again and again until I can love myself because you have loved me, loved me enough to give your life for mine. When I receive you in the Eucharist, it is easy to be distracted or bored. Jesus! Impress on me how close you are at this precious moment. Break through my inner barriers with your intimate personal presence. Amen.

Contemplatio

You know me and you love me.

Good Friday

⁝ ⋯⋯⋯⋯ ⁝

Lectio

John 18:1–19:42

Meditatio

> *"I thirst...."*

So much has been written about the Passion in the last 2,000 years. What more can be said? Even more, how can words describe everything that the words "Good Friday" encompass and all that Jesus suffered for us? Perhaps Jesus' cry, "I thirst," best captures the human and divine pathos of this day. All of us know what thirst is. Did Jesus only mean that he thirsted for something to drink? Or was he thirsting for much more? What was Jesus really saying with these two poignant words? What resounding significance these words have! They declare that Jesus, the Son of God, had so completely been stripped of everything that he could not even alleviate his own thirst.

Was he expressing the thirst of God the Father for the restoration of our ruptured relationship? Was Jesus thirsting to taste once more the food of the kingdom of heaven, where he would enjoy the presence of not only his Father, but ours as well?

What will my response be? How will I alleviate Jesus' thirst? Will I understand it simply as a cry for something to drink—a desire that an immediate human need be satiated? Can I hear Jesus cry out these words in the depths of my heart, allow them to reverberate in the hollow of my own abyss, and hear in the echo an invitation? Will this invitation become a point of continual intimacy with myself and Jesus, so that his death is truly the consummation of his life and mine?

The litmus test of my response will not be an abstract internal affair. Rather, it will take flesh in the way I respond to the cry of thirst from those in my life, a cry that is often suffocated. If I can hear the undertones of Jesus' cry of thirst, I may be able to hear my own and others' unspoken thirst. Such a thirst can only be satiated by one gift—me.

Oratio

Jesus, I see you naked, bloody, suffering terribly. You cry out in pain and agony. I hear you say, "I thirst." I feel helpless because I don't know what you mean. How do you want me to alleviate your thirst? I need help getting in touch with my own thirst—a thirst that I unconsciously fill with so many distractions that leave me unsatisfied. I thirst. I thirst. I thirst. I know most of all, Lord, that I thirst for love. Could that be what you ultimately thirst for, too? Then help me fall in love with you. Amen.

Contemplatio

"Let anyone who thirsts come to me and drink" (Jn 7:37).

Easter Vigil — A

∴ ··········· ∴

Lectio

Matthew 28:1–10

Meditatio

> *"Do not be afraid! I know that you are seeking Jesus the crucified.*
> *He is not here, for he has been raised just as he said."*

Alleluia! Christ is risen! Alleluia!

Our long Lenten journey has led us, at last, to the joy of the resurrection. In Matthew's account, we find two women, Mary Magdalene and the other Mary, going to the tomb of Jesus. Matthew notes that the first day of the week was dawning. The new creation has begun. The language of this Gospel passage also points out that Jesus' resurrection is an earth-shattering event. The mention of the earthquake, the glorious angel, and the appearance of Jesus, risen and glorified, all serve to underline that the new creation has dawned.

Both the angel and Jesus tell the two Marys to go and bring the good news to the disciples. Mary Magdalene has been called "the apostle to the apostles," because she saw the risen Jesus before they did and ran to tell them about it. The women were so overjoyed that they could not help but burst out and tell the good news.

That same task awaits us today. Many people have still not heard the Good News of Jesus Christ. Faith is a gift that grows when it is shared. You never know what will happen when you speak to others about Jesus. Here is one example. Recently two sisters from my community had done some evangelization work at a nearby parish. They provided some good Catholic reading materials and gave some talks on prayer. It just so happened that when two other sisters were out on an errand, a man came up to them on the street and told them he had attended the parish mission. He said that he hadn't been praying for many years, but the sisters' talk inspired him to take it up again. "My life has been transformed," he said simply. Then he told them he had gotten help for a drinking problem and felt more peace and happiness than he had in years. This is the power of Jesus' resurrection in our everyday lives!

Oratio

Jesus, thank you for dying on the cross for us and bringing us new life through your resurrection. Show us the power of the resurrection in our lives today. When we meet troubles along the way, help us to see beyond them and trust that you are with us. Show us your power and help us to live always in the joy of Easter. Give us the courage to speak to others about the good news. May our lives bear witness to you and light the way for others.

Contemplatio

"Behold, I have told you."

Easter Vigil — B

⁝ ⋯⋯⋯⋯ ⁝

Lectio

Mark 16:1–7

Meditatio

> *"Do not be amazed! You seek Jesus of Nazareth, the crucified.
> He has been raised; he is not here."*

The sun was just inching its way over the horizon when the women sought to anoint you, Lord. Their love for you pushed aside any apprehension they must have felt at seeing the stone rolled away. Your messenger, the young man in white, told them *the Good News:* "The Crucified has been raised!" They saw the empty space where your body lay on Good Friday evening. They believed and were immediately commissioned: "go and tell" the apostles that Jesus is alive and "you will see him, as he told you."

Lord, I often take this Good News for granted. Your paschal mystery encompasses your saving passion, death and resurrection. Sometimes I fall into a sort of spiritual denial by resenting opportunities to share in the first two parts of your paschal mystery. My sufferings and the little "deaths" of daily living pull a thick curtain over the window of my soul. When your grace reminds me of the resurrection, it pulls aside that curtain and floods my soul with the light of resurrection hope and joy. Of all the days of the year, today is a day to "rejoice and be glad." Your resurrection erases all fear. It's the bedrock of my faith. As Saint Paul says, without the resurrection, our faith would be in vain (see I Cor 15:17). Two millennia of martyrs and saints, a true "cloud of witnesses," have gone before us and invite me to join them. Like the holy women, I too am entrusted with the message "to go and tell" the consoling news that death is not the end, but the beginning of eternal life.

Oratio

Lord Jesus, I kneel in awe before your tomb. I do believe in your resurrection and in my resurrection in the life to come! Thank you for your resurrection that roots me in Christian hope. Demolish the tomb of my woundedness, regrets, and bad habits. Let me look beyond myself to see those longing to hear the Good News from my lips, to see Good News in my actions and my conviction. Let me be aware of those next to me longing for your Good News. May my life be a sign of hope for all to see, and a song of thanksgiving for your dying and rising. Amen.

Contemplatio

He has been raised.... He is going before you.

Easter Vigil — C

:• ·········· •:

Lectio

Luke 24:1–12

Meditatio

"And they remembered."

It was barely morning. Had those women moving purposefully toward the tomb even slept? What was the sign that it was dawn and not still night? Numb with grief, the women were intent on their labor of love, their final act of reverence and respect. They had work to do! First things first!

Who were these women who came to anoint the defiled body of a crucified man? "The women were Mary Magdalene, Joanna, and Mary the mother of James," Luke tells us. But they were not alone. "Why do you seek the living one among the dead. . . . Remember what he said to you while he was still in Galilee. . . ." the mysterious messengers said at Jesus' empty tomb.

Memory is one of the key concepts of the entire Bible, from "Remember the marvels the Lord has done" (Ps 107) to "Do this in memory of me" (Lk 22:19). At the center of this evening's Easter Gospel is a single, utterly essential word: "Remember."

"And they remembered."

There is something remarkable about that remembering. It gave them the interpretive key for the whole bewildering set of experiences they had been through that week. On the power of their restored memory and all that it revealed, the women went to the eleven apostles with a world-changing message. Once they remembered the words Jesus had spoken, the women had everything they needed: they had found the Good News and became the first ones to proclaim it.

The grace we remember tonight is not confined to the past, whether it is the grace of the Lord's own dying and rising, or grace shown to me, personally, transforming my life under some crucial aspect. The Easter season, which begins in the darkness of this "most blessed of all nights," can be the beginning of fifty days of blessed memory.

Oratio

Lord, the call to remember awakens my mind to a time when your grace was especially present and powerful in my life.... That grace is not locked in the tomb of time: it is still alive, still present, still active, because it is *your* grace. Throughout the Easter season, renew me daily in the memory of all you have done in my life, so that I can give you daily thanks and praise!

Contemplatio

I will remember all your wonderful deeds!

Easter Sunday

∴ ············ ∴

Lectio

John 20:1–9

Meditatio

> *"Mary of Magdala came to the tomb early in the morning,*
> *while it was still dark. . . ."*

Still dark. Darkness shrouds the earth, dawn has not broken, and the light of faith has not yet risen in Mary Magdalene's heart. The night still seems to reign, yet this is illusion! Something unforeseen, new, living—pulsing with hope—has emptied the tomb of death in the night.

Mary is shocked. Nothing is as it was, yet she does not yet understand what is to be. The idea of Christ alive—*risen!*— is still unthinkable, beyond possibility. Mary *runs* to the disciples not in hope, but in desperation: *"They have taken the Lord from the tomb, and we don't know where they put him."* She *runs* in fear, believing the tomb has been raided, the body of one she loves stolen in the night. She *runs*, because she cannot face this alone.

Why do our hearts resist resurrection? Why can't we grasp the possibility of new life? Sometimes, it's harder to embrace resurrection than the cross! Why? What keeps us from seeing and believing, as John does?

Perhaps it is because accepting resurrection means accepting all that came before it. All the pain, chaos, and confusion were necessary in order to bring us this new life of joy, freedom, and hope. *The resurrection cannot exist without the cross.* We rebel against this reality. Yet it remains true, both in the life of Christ, and in our own lives. Somehow, it is often in our times of deepest darkness, in the secretive silence of the tomb, that Christ brings us the most profound gifts of grace, insight, maturation, and growth. Jesus then comes and raids our tombs of death with his new life! And we find that we are a new creation. *We are utterly transformed!*

We may at times find ourselves with Mary, weeping before an empty tomb. Yet we know that in a few short hours, Mary's profound grief and fear will give way to profound wonder, joy, and awe!

Oratio

Jesus, what was it like for the disciples that first Easter morning? I can only imagine! To have one's sense of loss and fear unexpectedly overcome by the unprecedented moment of resurrection! Jesus, I know you are at work in my life, too, opening long-sealed tombs and bringing new life. Open my eyes to the glory of your resurrection within and around me. Help me to see and believe. And, in believing, may my spirit be disposed to receive the true joy and peace you bring. For your love has conquered death!

Contemplatio

Lord, I believe!

Alleluia!
Love, life, and light have overcome
hate, death, and darkness — forever!
Alleluia!

The Exsultet

:• ·········· •:

Rejoice, heavenly powers! Sing, choirs of angels!
Exult, all creation around God's throne!
Jesus Christ, our King, is risen!
Sound the trumpet of salvation!
Rejoice, O earth, in shining splendor,
radiant in the brightness of your King!
Christ has conquered! Glory fills you!
Darkness vanishes forever!
Rejoice, O Mother Church! Exult in glory!
The risen Savior shines upon you!
Let this place resound with joy,
echoing the mighty song of all God's people! ...
It is truly right
that with full hearts and minds and voices
we should praise the unseen God, the all-powerful Father,
and his only Son, our Lord Jesus Christ.
For Christ has ransomed us with his blood,
and paid for us the price of Adam's sin
to our eternal Father!
This is our Passover feast,
when Christ, the true Lamb, is slain,
whose blood consecrates the homes of all believers.
This is the night when first you saved our fathers:
you freed the people of Israel from their slavery
and led them dry-shod through the sea.
This is the night when Christians everywhere,

washed clean of sin
and freed from all defilement,
are restored to grace and grow together in holiness.
This is the night when Jesus Christ
broke the chains of death
and rose triumphant from the grave.
Father, how wonderful your care for us!
How boundless your merciful love!
To ransom a slave
you gave away your Son.
O happy fault, O necessary sin of Adam,
which gained for us so great a Redeemer!
The power of this holy night
dispels all evil, washes guilt away,
restores lost innocence, brings mourners joy;
it casts out hatred, brings us peace, and humbles earthly
        pride.
Night truly blessed when heaven is wedded to earth
and man is reconciled with God!
Therefore, heavenly Father, in the joy of this night,
receive our evening sacrifice of praise,
your Church's solemn offering.
Accept this Easter candle,
[a flame divided but undimmed,
a pillar of fire that glows to the honor of God.]
May it always dispel the darkness of this night!
May the Morning Star which never sets find this flame
        still burning:
Christ, that Morning Star, who came back from the dead,
and shed his peaceful light on all mankind,
your Son who lives and reigns for ever and ever.

Monday in the Octave of Easter

∴ ⋯⋯⋯⋯ ∴

Lectio

The Exsultet (p. 132)

Meditatio

"Rejoice, heavenly powers!"

At the Easter Vigil, Saturday night, we listened to the chanting of the Exsultet—a beautiful poem announcing Jesus' resurrection from the dead. It is the end of a long night for fallen humanity and the beginning of a freedom we could not imagine.

The first three words of the Exsultet invite all of heaven to join with us in singing out our joy. The love and mercy of God have shown themselves stronger than the worst that the world can do. Our gratitude is not enough. We want to combine our words of joy and praise with those of all of heaven and earth!

Of course, the liturgies of Easter are filled with so much high-pitched joy, but our own lives may be abruptly returning to normal on this day after Easter. Work, school, or family concerns suddenly make the celebration of Easter seem remote. The energy of the Easter Vigil seems quickly dissipated.

How can we keep the joy of the resurrection fresh in our hearts? We begin today by joining our own voices in prayer with the prayer of the entire Body of Christ—and indeed, all the heavenly powers. As we pray during the next few days with the words of the Exsultet, we return in our hearts to the moment of the Easter proclamation. This octave of Easter is a time to revel in the assurance that, ultimately, love and life triumph over all darkness.

Oratio

Lord, as the Church continues to celebrate your resurrection with enthusiastic joy, I am returning to my ordinary routine. Light the flame of your Easter fire in my heart, so that I might unite my voice in prayer with your sons and daughters everywhere. Keep this fire of love and joy burning in my heart always.

Contemplatio

"This is the day the LORD has made; let us rejoice in it and be glad" (Ps 118:24).

Tuesday in the Octave of Easter

$\vdots$ .... $\vdots$

Lectio

The Exsultet (p. 132)

Meditatio

"Darkness vanishes forever!"

The transition from darkness to light is one of my favorite parts of the Easter Vigil. Standing outside in the dark, waiting for the Vigil to begin, I can't help but feel a sense of relief. Holy Week can feel so intense—even heavy—as we read over and over the story of Jesus' passion. It's a story full of darkness, but I want to hear that the story is not over yet. In New England, where I live, the dark night of the Vigil is often cold as well. The warmth *and* the light of the new fire add to the sense of anticipation. Soon, very soon, we will be indoors, lights ablaze, bells ringing, singing the Gloria amidst lilies, incense, and trumpets. The darkness has vanished.

My own life can be like this, too. Sometimes I live my own little Lent, a time that seems to be filled with more than the usual difficulties or challenges. The pain and intensity of Holy Week can be a part of our lives as well, when it seems that the worst has happened. We may sense how the apostles might have felt—that things were not supposed to work out this way. But Easter reminds me that the story doesn't end with these moments. Easter gives me hope that the darkness will give way to light.

Sometimes the light flashes for a moment, only to be dimmed—like Lent returning each year. But in Jesus' resurrection, life and light overcome all obstacles. We are promised that our Lents and Good Fridays, our moments of suffering, failure, betrayal, or pain, do not have the last word.

Walking in out of the cold, holding my newly lit candle, listening to these words of the Exsultet, I am given a taste of the love and mercy of God, which casts out darkness. This is the hope that sustains us each day.

Oratio

Jesus, as we celebrate your resurrection, renew your hope in my heart. During these days of light and rejoicing, fill me with your strength to carry me through difficulty. May your resurrection help me to see the events of my life with new eyes and to trust in your promise of new life.

Contemplatio

"[T]ake courage; I have conquered the world!" (Jn 16:33)

Wednesday in the Octave of Easter

❖ ⋯⋯⋯⋯ ❖

Lectio

The Exsultet (p. 132)

Meditatio

"This is the night. . . ."

When we think of Easter, most likely we think of Easter Sunday morning, Easter egg hunts, Easter bunnies, Easter candy, Easter clothes, Easter Sunday Mass.... The Exsultet, however, takes us back to the night, to several important nights in the history of the world: the night of Passover, when the angel of death passed over the houses of the Israelites who had marked the lintels of their doors with the blood of the lamb; the night of the Exodus, when God saved our fathers and freed Israel from slavery; the night when Jesus Christ broke the chains of death, rising triumphantly from the grave.

Easter is about remembering these important nights. If we forget them, we forget who we are—who we have been made to be through the life, death, and resurrection of the Son of God, the Lamb of God, who loved us and gave his life for us.

These nights have something in common: they are nights when God acted powerfully to free people he chose from situations of slavery and imprisonment. The Israelites had been in Egypt for 400 years, reduced to pitiful, miserable slavery under the Egyptian lash. God intervened on behalf of this people. He invited them into a love relationship with him. He promised to protect and cherish them, if they desired to be a faithful people dedicated entirely to his love and worship. Of course, at that point, the newly freed slaves were full of promises about their fidelity to this God who was working on their behalf. These promises eventually disintegrated to mediocrity, indifference, forgetfulness, and finally idolatry. No matter how much God called out to them, they insisted on giving themselves to other gods.

The night of the resurrection was an exodus in which Jesus himself came to lead us out of this slavery of sin and death, this hopeless adultery; to walk before us, with us, in us, and for us to the Father. This night, every Easter Vigil night, we are connected to the ongoing, perpetual, dynamic movement of exodus that frees us and weds us to God.

Oratio

God, as I enjoy the Easter candy and Easter egg hunts, help me remember who I am. Don't let me settle for the mediocrity of consumerism, compulsion, indifference, or boredom. Because of "this night," wake my heart to a selfless concern for others, simplicity, gratuitousness, and a real dedication to the joy of others. Amen.

Contemplatio

Jesus, I remember who I am.

Thursday in the Octave of Easter

∴ ⋯⋯⋯⋯ ∴

Lectio

The Exsultet (p. 132)

Meditatio

> *"Night truly blessed when heaven is wedded to earth."*

I had a dream recently in which Jesus seemed to say to me, "What do I want? Now I only want a deep love between us. I want you to tell me over and over again that you love me." It has taken me half a lifetime to know in the core of my being that God is only interested in love. I have kept myself a safe distance from God by labeling, judging, and analyzing myself. I have shut God out by self-absorption and self-protection. But God isn't interested in remembering all that. He just rings my doorbell and says, "Now the winter is past. My only interest is in you loving me."

How do we so easily get it wrong? We think Christianity is about rules. We tell others that Christianity is about keeping the rules, repenting of breaking them, resolving to abide by them. But we instinctively know that rule-keeping isn't what it's all about. The Fathers of the Church knew it. They said God came into this world for a *marriage*. The night of the resurrection is proclaimed in the Exsultet as a night truly blessed, for heaven is wedded to earth. The joy in marriage celebrations, the love between bride and groom, overpowers lesser loves, self-loves. This love for a lifetime needs to be tended. It doesn't just happen. It cost Jesus his life to establish a covenant in which we would begin to live no longer for ourselves but for him and for one another. He is the bridge between heaven and earth, Creator and creature. In Jesus, God has cast his fortunes with us. And he asks me, "Will you tell me that you love me?" It's that simple.

What would happen if the sacrament of Reconciliation was about reconciling lovers? The greatest sin is having forgotten to love, being too busy to love, being too important to love, refusing to love. When we really know deep inside how much we have been loved, we will be too eager to tell Jesus of our desire to love him to stay away from the sacraments of Reconciliation and the Eucharist.

Oratio

Jesus, in the center of my being, I am aware of a new thirst for you, for love, aware of a trembling hope that at last what I have found might be true: I am loved and all you want is my love. Let us jump into each other's arms, trusting this love, renewing it moment by moment, day by day for a lifetime. Amen.

Contemplatio

The winter is past. Today I begin to love you.

Friday in the Octave of Easter

∴ ⋯⋯⋯⋯ ∴

Lectio

The Exsultet (p. 132)

Meditatio

"A flame divided but undimmed...."

The Easter candle was lit from the blessed fire at the beginning of the Easter Vigil. Then from that one flame, all the candles of the people were lit. As we stood facing the Easter candle, holding our own small candles, the Exsultet was proclaimed. The sharing of the flame that results in many points of light is a sign of something deeper: the light of Christ. The light we carry into the world—the light of our faith, the joy and love we bring to others—has its source in the light of Christ. We don't light our own candles. We share the light of Christ. Or rather, he shares his light with us.

With most sharing, something is lost and less is left, even though the heart often receives back more than the hands gave away. But for Jesus it's different. The ocean of his love is infinitely vast; his well is infinitely deep; his flame is eternally burning. If we share from him, we will be able to give and give and not be any less. If in our giving we find that we quickly run out of hope and love to offer others, perhaps we are trying to draw on our own store and not on that of Jesus.

Any good we can do in this world is from him. If we can help anyone, it is Jesus working through us. Any good intention we have, and any hope for transformation and growth, is a gift from God. We know these are not our doing because they are beyond our power. It's when we forget that and think that we *create* the flame that we use to light others' candles ("Oh, the poor things, sitting there in the dark—I must go and rescue them") that we quickly burn up and burn out.

Christ is our light! Thanks be to God!

Oratio

Jesus, my faith, hope, and love are gifts from you. Help me remember that, especially when I feel you nudging me to use them to do good for someone. I know that in order to persevere in any kind of help of others, I must always come back to you. You fan my embers back into flame, or even relight my candle if it goes out.

If I remember this, I will also not make the mistake of leading people to myself instead of to you.

Contemplatio

Jesus, true light of the world.

Saturday in the Octave of Easter

∴ ············ ∴

Lectio

The Exsultet (p. 132)

Meditatio

> *"May the Morning Star which never sets*
> *find this flame still burning."*

The real joy of the resurrection and of the Easter Season is knowing that just as Jesus was raised from the dead, we too will be raised from the dead. Our true happiness is the knowledge that this risen Lord raises others from their darkness—the darkness of sin or doubt, confusion or self-hatred. The darkness has been pierced with the flame of the Paschal candle, and the cosmic darkness has been overtaken by the power of the Light of the World.

If we are but onlookers to the death and resurrection of Jesus, participating in the liturgical celebrations of the Easter Triduum and the fifty days of Easter in *memory* of the One who lived a distant 2,000 years ago, we will be inwardly untouched by it all. We participate in inspiring liturgies but we do not have to bind ourselves to anything. But if we pledge ourselves to the crucified God, to the risen Savior, to share in his death and in his life, with our eyes on the things that are above, both in the liturgy and in the difficulties of daily life, we participate in the powerful love of Jesus, who took what was negative in this world and transformed it into glory by the power of his vulnerable love.

With Easter, God begins the re-creation of the world, transforming it in the image of his Son. We are ambassadors of this new creation, of this completely overpowering love affair that God has with us, his longing for us to return this love. This is the mission of the Church—to be as the first disciples, so overjoyed at seeing their Master again that they run to tell the others, that they spend their lives telling and writing what they have seen and heard, unable to be silent, even in the face of martyrdom. Easter is not about lilies and trumpets and bonnets. It sets us on the serious road of discipleship and mission for the sake of the world that still waits to hear that Jesus has risen from the dead!

Oratio

Risen Savior, fill me with your Spirit, send me forth to my family, to my neighbors, to my parish, to my country, to my school, to my office ... on the road, in the car, at meetings, cooking supper, making decisions ... forgiving, loving, remembering, desiring, learning, starting again and again ... so that all may know that "Jesus Christ is Lord."

Contemplatio

"Jesus Christ is Lord!"

List of Contributers

:• ·········· •:

RECOMMENDED READING

Sr. Elena Bosetti's contemplative reading of the Gospels

Luke: The Song of God's Mercy
0-8198-4521-3
$12.95

Mark: The Risk of Believing
0-8198-4847-6
$12.95

Matthew: The Journey Toward Hope
0-8198-4848-4
$15.95

New volume on the Gospel of John, coming soon!

Scripture scholar Elena Bosetti brings a prayerful and deeply human perspective to God's Word. Very helpful reading for those who would like to continue doing *lectio divina* on the Gospels.

Order at www.pauline.org, or by calling Pauline Books & Media at 1-800-876-4463, or through the book and media center nearest you.

Make this Advent a favorable time of grace by praying *lectio divina* with the Daughters of St. Paul.

Advent Grace: Daily Gospel Reflections
By the Daughters of St. Paul
0-8198-0787-7
$7.95

Order at www.pauline.org, or by calling Pauline Books & Media at 1-800-876-4463, or through the book and media center nearest you.

BOOKS & MEDIA

A mission of the Daughters of St. Paul

As apostles of Jesus Christ, evangelizing today's world:

We are CALLED to holiness
by God's living Word and Eucharist.

We COMMUNICATE the Gospel message
through our lives and through all
available forms of media.

We SERVE the Church
by responding to the hopes and needs
of all people with the Word of God,
in the spirit of St. Paul.

For more information visit our website:
www.pauline.org.

BOOKS & MEDIA

The Daughters of St. Paul operate book and media centers at the following addresses. Visit, call or write the one nearest you today, or find us on the World Wide Web, www.pauline.org

CALIFORNIA
3908 Sepulveda Blvd, Culver City, CA 90230	310-397-8676
2650 Broadway Street, Redwood City, CA 94063	650-369-4230
5945 Balboa Avenue, San Diego, CA 92111	858-565-9181

FLORIDA
145 S.W. 107th Avenue, Miami, FL 33174	305-559-6715

HAWAII
1143 Bishop Street, Honolulu,HI 96813	808-521-2731
Neighbor Islands call:	866-521-2731

ILLINOIS
172 North Michigan Avenue, Chicago, IL 60601	312-346-4228

LOUISIANA
4403 Veterans Memorial Blvd, Metairie, LA 70006	504-887-7631

MASSACHUSETTS
885 Providence Hwy, Dedham, MA 02026	781-326-5385

MISSOURI
9804 Watson Road, St. Louis, MO 63126	314-965-3512

NEW JERSEY
561 U.S. Route 1, Wick Plaza, Edison, NJ 08817	732-572-1200

NEW YORK
150 East 52nd Street, New York, NY 10022	212-754-1110

PENNSYLVANIA
9171-A Roosevelt Blvd, Philadelphia, PA 19114	215-676-9494

SOUTH CAROLINA
243 King Street, Charleston,SC 29401	843-577-0175

TENNESSEE
4811 Poplar Avenue, Memphis, TN 38117	901-761-2987

TEXAS
114 Main Plaza, San Antonio, TX 78205	210-224-8101

VIRGINIA
1025 King Street, Alexandria, VA 22314	703-549-3806

CANADA
3022 Dufferin Street, Toronto, ON M6B 3T5	416-781-9131

¡También somos su fuente para libros, videos
y música en español!

W9-AKC-638

The Compassionate Life

Tenzin Gyatso
THE FOURTEENTH DALAI LAMA

Wisdom Publications • Boston

Wisdom Publications, Inc.
199 Elm Street, Somerville MA 02144 USA
www.wisdompubs.org

© 2001 Tenzin Gyatso, the Fourteenth Dalai Lama
All rights reserved.

Verses from the *Guide to the Bodhisattva's Way of Life* are adapted from the
translation by Stephen Batchelor (Library of Tibetan Works and Archives,
1979). The translation of *Eight Verses for Training the Mind* is courtesy of
John D. Dunne.

No part of this book may be reproduced in any form or by any means, elec-
tronic or mechanical, including photocopying, recording, or by any information storage and retrieval system or technologies now known or later
developed, without permission in writing from the publisher.

Library of Congress Cataloging-in-Publication Data
Bstan-'dzin-rgya-mtsho, Dalai Lama XIV, 1935–
        The compassionate life / Tenzin Gyatso.
          p.   cm.
        Includes index.
        ISBN 0-86171-301-x (alk. paper)
          1. Compassion—Religious aspects—Buddhism.
        2. Religious life—Buddhism. I. Title.
        BQ4360.B75 2001
        294.3'5677—dc21   2001026867

06 05 04 03 02   6 5 4 3

Cover photo by William Yang. Reproduced courtesy of FPMT
Australia. Interior photos by Ueli Minder. Designed by Gopa.

Wisdom Publications' books are printed on acid-free paper and meet the
guidelines for permanence and durability set by the Committee on Production Guidelines for Book Longevity of the Council on Library Resources.

Printed in the United States of America.

Table of Contents

Publisher's Acknowledgment

THE PUBLISHER gratefully acknowledges the generous help of Richard Gere and the Gere Foundation in sponsoring the publication of this book.

Editor's Preface

IN HIS NUMEROUS PUBLIC APPEARANCES, His Holiness the Dalai Lama always returns to the topic of compassion. Compassion, or the desire to remove the suffering of another, is of course a central ideal for the practicing Buddhist. But one does not need to spend much time observing His Holiness to realize that his commitment to this virtue goes far beyond mere religious obligation. In his simple yet inimitable way, the Dalai Lama displays a profound recognition of the power of human affection in addressing the world's most urgent and complex problems.

At first glance, the Dalai Lama's rhetoric may seem almost naive, uninformed by a grasp of real-world politics and the subtleties of the human heart. Upon deeper inspection, however, it becomes clear that His Holiness speaks from a deep well of experience, grounded in his systematic training as a Buddhist monk and his personal experiences

as the political and religious leader of the Tibetan people. His compassion is not timid or vague; it is solid, resolute, and above all wise.
The difference is that His Holiness understands the mind—the power
of our thoughts and emotions in shaping reality. He sees the precise
relationship between the motivation we have and the results we get,
and his life exemplifies the depth of his recognition.

It is our hope at Wisdom Publications that the teachings we have
woven together to make this book will help advance His Holiness'
own goals for world peace, religious tolerance, and spiritual development, while providing effective tools for those interested in cultivating lives of greater compassion.

David Kittelstrom

The Compassionate Life

1

The Benefits of Compassion

Y EXPERIENCES are nothing special, just ordinary human ones. Through my Buddhist training, however, I have learned something about compassion and developing a good heart, and that experience has proved very helpful in my day-to-day life. For example, the region of Tibet I come from is called Amdo, and people usually regard people who come from Amdo as short-tempered. So in Tibet, when someone would lose his or her temper, people would often take it as a sign that the person was from Amdo! However, when I compare my temperament now to the way it was when I was between the ages of fifteen and twenty, I see a noticeable difference. These days, I hardly find myself being irritated at all, and even when I am, it doesn't last long. This is a marvelous benefit of my own practice and training—now I am always quite cheerful!

In my lifetime, I have lost my country and have been reduced to being totally dependent on the goodwill of others. I have also lost my mother, and most of my tutors and lamas have passed away. Of course, these are tragic incidents, and I feel sad when I think about them. However, I don't feel overwhelmed by sadness. Old, familiar faces disappear and new faces appear, but I still maintain my happiness and peace of mind. This capacity to relate to events from a broader perspective is, for me, one of the marvels of human nature, and I believe it is rooted in our capacity for compassion and kindness toward others.

✤ OUR FUNDAMENTAL NATURE

Some of my friends have told me that while love and compassion are marvelous and good, they are not really very relevant. Our world, they say, is not a place where such virtues have much influence or power. They claim that anger and hatred are so much a part of human nature that humanity will always be dominated by them. I do not agree.

We humans have existed in our present form for about a hundred thousand years. I believe that if during this time the human mind had been primarily controlled by anger and hatred, our population would have decreased. But today, despite all our wars, we find that the human population is greater than ever. This clearly indicates to me that while anger and aggression are surely present, love and compassion predominate in the world. This is why what we call "news" is composed of mostly unpleasant or tragic events; compassionate activities are so much a part of daily life that they are taken for granted and therefore are largely ignored.

If we look at basic human nature, we can see that it is more gentle than aggressive. For example, if we examine various animals, we notice that animals of a more peaceful nature have a corresponding body structure, whereas predatory animals have a body structure that has developed according to their nature. Compare the tiger and the deer: there are great differences in their physical structures. When we compare our own body structure to theirs, we see that we resemble deer and rabbits more than tigers. Even our teeth are more like a rabbit's, are they not? They are not like a tiger's. Our fingernails are another good example—I cannot even harm a rat with a swipe of my fingernails alone. Of course, because of human intelligence, we are able to devise and use various tools and methods to accomplish things that would be difficult to accomplish without them. But because of our physical situation we belong to the gentle-animal category.

We are, after all, social animals. Without human friendship, without the human smile, our lives become miserable. The loneliness becomes unbearable. Such human interdependence is a natural law— that is to say, according to natural law, we depend on others to live.

If, under certain circumstances, because something is wrong inside us, our attitude toward our fellow human beings on whom we depend becomes hostile, how can we hope to attain peace of mind or a happy life? According to basic human nature or natural law, interdependence—giving and receiving affection—is the key to happiness.

This fact may become more evident if we reflect on the basic pattern of our existence. In order to do more than just barely survive, we need shelter, food, companions, friends, the esteem of others, resources, and so on; these things do not come about from ourselves alone but are all dependent on others. Suppose one single person were to live alone in a remote and uninhabited place. No matter how strong, healthy, or educated this person were, there would be no possibility of his or her leading a happy and fulfilling existence. If a person is living, for example, somewhere deep in the African jungle and is the only human being in an animal sanctuary, given that person's intelligence and cunning, the best he or she can do is to become, perhaps, king of the jungle. Can such a person have friends? Acquire renown? Can this person become a hero if he or she wishes to become one? I think the answer to all these questions is a definite no, for all these factors come about only in relation to other fellow humans.

When you are young, healthy, and strong, you sometimes can get the feeling that you are totally independent and do not need anyone else. But this is an illusion. Even at that prime age of your life, simply because your are a human being, you need friends, don't you? This is especially true when we become old. For example, in my own case, the Dalai Lama, who is now in his sixties, is beginning to show various signs of approaching old age. I can see the appearance of more white hair on my head, and I am also starting to experience problems sometimes with the knees when getting up or sitting down. As we grow old, we need to rely more and more on the help of others: this is the nature of our lives as human beings.

In at least one sense, we can say that other people are really the principal source of all our experiences of joy, happiness, and prosperity, and not only in terms of our day-to-day dealings with people. We can see that all the desirable experiences that we cherish or aspire to attain are dependent upon cooperation and interaction with others. It is an obvious fact. Similarly, from the point of view of a Buddhist practitioner, many of the high levels of realization that you gain and the progress that you make on your spiritual journey are dependent upon cooperation and interaction with others. Furthermore, at the stage of complete enlightenment, the compassionate activities of a buddha can come about spontaneously only in relation to other beings, for those beings are the recipients and beneficiaries of those enlightened activities.

Even from a totally selfish perspective—wanting only our own happiness, comfort, and satisfaction in life, with no consideration of others' welfare—I would still argue that the fulfillment of our aspirations depends upon others. Even the committing of harmful actions depends on the existence of others. For example, in order to cheat, you need someone as the object of your act.

All events and incidents in life are so intimately linked with the fate of others that a single person on his or her own cannot even begin to act. Many ordinary human activities, both positive and negative, cannot even be conceived of apart from the existence of other people. Because of others, we have the opportunity to earn money if that is what we desire in life. Similarly, in reliance upon the existence of others it becomes possible for the media to create fame or disrepute for someone. On your own you cannot create any fame or disrepute no matter how loud you might shout. The closest you can get is to create an echo of your own voice.

Thus interdependence is a fundamental law of nature. Not only higher forms of life but also many of the smallest insects are social beings who, without any religion, law, or education, survive by mutual cooperation based on an innate recognition of their interconnectedness. The most subtle level of material phenomena is also governed by interdependence. All phenomena, from the planet we inhabit to the oceans, clouds, forests, and flowers that surround us, arise in dependence upon subtle patterns of energy. Without their proper interaction, they dissolve and decay.

❧ OUR NEED FOR LOVE

One great question underlies our experience, whether we think about it consciously or not: What is the purpose of life? I believe that our life's purpose is to be happy. From the moment of birth, every human being wants happiness and does not want suffering. Neither social conditioning, nor education, nor ideology affect this. From the very core of our being, we simply desire contentment. I don't know whether the universe, with its countless galaxies, stars, and planets, has a deeper meaning or not, but at the very least, it is clear that we humans who live on this earth face the task of making a happy life for ourselves.

We are not like machine-made objects. We are more than just matter; we have feelings and experiences. If we were merely mechanical entities, then machines themselves could alleviate all of our suffering and fulfill all our needs. But material comfort alone is not enough. No material object, however beautiful or valuable, can make us feel loved. We need something deeper, what I usually refer to as human affection. With human affection, or compassion, all the material advantages that we have at our disposal can be very constructive and can produce good results. Without human affection, however, material advantages alone will not satisfy us, nor will they produce in us any measure of mental peace or happiness. In fact, material advantages without human affection may even create additional problems. So when we consider our origins and our nature we discover that no one is born free from the need for love. And although some modern schools of thought seek to do so, human beings cannot be defined as solely physical.

Ultimately, the reason why love and compassion bring the greatest happiness is simply that our nature cherishes them above all else. However capable and skillful an individual may be, left alone, he or she will not survive. However vigorous and independent we may feel during the most prosperous periods of life, when we are sick, or very young or very old, we depend on the support of others. Let's look more closely at the ways that affection and compassion help us throughout our lives.

Our beliefs may differ when it comes to questions of the creation and evolution of our universe, but we can at least agree that each of us is the product of our own parents. In general, our conception took place not just in the context of sexual desire but also from our parents' decision to have a child. Such decisions are founded on responsibility and altruism—the parents' compassionate commitment to care for their child until it is able to take care of itself. Thus, from the very moment of our conception, our parents' love is directly involved in our creation.

I learned from meeting with some scientists, especially those working in the field of neurobiology, that there is strong scientific evidence to suggest that even in pregnancy a mother's state of mind, be it calm or agitated, has a great effect on the physical and mental well-being of the unborn child. It seems vital for the mother to maintain a calm and relaxed state of mind. After birth, the first few weeks are the most crucial period for the healthy development of the child. During this time, I was told, one of the most important factors for ensuring rapid and healthy growth of the baby's brain is the mother's constant physical touch. If the child is left unattended and uncared for during this critical period, although the effects on the child's mental well-being may not be immediately obvious, physical damage can result from this that will later become quite noticeable.

The central importance of love and caring continues throughout childhood. When a child sees someone with an open and affectionate demeanor, someone who is smiling or has a loving and caring expression, the child naturally feels happy and protected. On the other hand, if someone tries to hurt the child, it becomes gripped by fear, which leads to harmful consequences in terms of the child's development. Nowadays, many children grow up in unhappy homes. If they do not receive proper affection, in later life they will rarely love their parents and, not infrequently, will find it hard to love others. This is of course very sad.

As children grow older and enter school, their need for support must be met by their teachers. If a teacher not only imparts academic education but also assumes responsibility for preparing students for life, his or her pupils will feel trust and respect, and what has been taught will leave an indelible impression on their minds. On the other hand, subjects taught by a teacher who does not show true concern for students' overall well-being will be regarded as temporary and will not be retained for long.

Similarly, if one is sick and being treated in hospital by a doctor who evinces a warm human feeling, one feels at ease, and the doctor's desire to give the best possible care is itself curative, irrespective of the degree of his or her technical skill. On the other hand, if one's doctor lacks human feeling and displays an unfriendly expression, impatience, or casual disregard, one will feel anxious, even if the person is the most highly qualified doctor and the disease has been correctly diagnosed and the right medication prescribed. Inevitably, patients' feelings make a difference to the quality and completeness of their recovery.

Even in ordinary conversation in everyday life, when someone speaks with warm human feeling, we enjoy listening and respond accordingly; the whole conversation becomes interesting, however unimportant the topic may be. On the other hand, if a person speaks coldly or harshly, we feel uneasy and wish for a quick end to the interaction. From the least important to the most important event, the affection and respect of others are vital for our happiness.

Recently I met another group of scientists in America who said that the rate of mental illness in their country was quite high, around 12 percent of the population. It became clear during our discussion that depression was caused not by a lack of material necessities but more likely by a difficulty in giving and receiving affection.

So, as you can see from all of this, whether or not we are consciously aware of it, from the day we are born, the need for human affection is in our very blood. Even if the affection comes from an animal or someone we would normally consider an enemy, both children and adults will naturally gravitate toward it.

❧ THE ULTIMATE SOURCE OF SUCCESS

As human beings we all have the potential to be happy and compassionate people, and we also have the potential to be miserable and harmful to others. The potential for all these things is present within each of us. If we want to be happy, then the important thing is to try to promote the positive and useful aspects in each of us and to try to reduce the negative. Doing negative things, such as stealing and lying, may occasionally seem to bring some short-term satisfaction, but in the long term they will always bring us misery. Positive acts always bring us inner strength. With inner strength we have less fear and more self-confidence, and it becomes much easier to extend our sense of caring to others without any barriers, whether religious, cultural, or otherwise. It is thus very important to recognize our potential for both good and bad, and then to observe and analyze it carefully.

This is what I call the promotion of human value. My main concern is always how to promote an understanding of deeper human value. This deeper human value is compassion, a sense of caring, and commitment. No matter what your religion, and whether you are a believer or a nonbeliever, without them you cannot be happy.

Let's examine the usefulness of compassion and a good heart in daily life. If we are in a good mood when we get up in the morning, if there is a warm-hearted feeling within, automatically our inner door is opened for that day. Even should an unfriendly person happen along, we would not experience much disturbance and might even manage to say something nice to that person. We could chat with the not-so-friendly person and perhaps even have a meaningful conversation. Once we create a friendly and positive atmosphere, it automatically helps to reduce fear and insecurity. In this way we can easily make more friends and create more smiles.

But on a day when our mood is less positive and we are feeling irritated, automatically our inner door closes. As a result, even if we encounter our best friend, we feel uncomfortable and strained. These instances show how our inner attitude makes a great difference in our daily experiences. In order to create a pleasant atmosphere within our-selves, within our families, within our communities, we have to real-ize that the ultimate source of that pleasant atmosphere is within the individual, within each of us—a good heart, human compassion, love.

Compassion doesn't have only mental benefits, but it con-tributes to good physical health as well. According to contemporary medicine, as well as to my personal experience, mental stability and physical well-being are directly related. Without question, anger and agitation make us more susceptible to illness. On the other hand, if the mind is tranquil and occupied with positive thoughts, the body will not easily fall prey to disease. This shows that the physical body itself appreciates and responds to human affection, human peace of mind.

Another thing that is quite clear to me is that the moment you think only of yourself, the focus of your whole reality narrows, and because of this narrow focus, uncomfortable things can appear huge and bring you fear and discomfort and a sense of feeling over-whelmed by misery. The moment you think of others with a sense of caring, however, your view widens. Within that wider perspective, your own problems appear to be of little significance, and this makes a big difference.

If you have a sense of caring for others, you will manifest a kind of inner strength in spite of your own difficulties and problems. With this strength, your own problems will seem less significant and bothersome to you. By going beyond your own problems and taking care of others, you gain inner strength, self-confidence, courage, and a greater sense of calm. This is a clear example of how one's way of thinking can really make a difference.

One's own self-interest and wishes are fulfilled as a byproduct of actually working for other sentient beings. As the well-known fifteenth-century master Tsongkhapa points out in his *Great Exposition of the Path to Enlightenment,* "The more the practitioner engages in activities and thoughts that are focused and directed toward the fulfillment of others' well-being, the fulfillment or realization of his or her own aspiration will come as a byproduct without having to make a separate effort." Some of you may have actually heard me remark, which I do quite often, that in some sense the bodhisattvas, the compassionate practitioners of the Buddhist path, are "wisely selfish" people, whereas people like us are the "foolishly selfish." We think of ourselves and disregard others, and the result is that we always remain unhappy and have a miserable time.

Other benefits of altruism and a good heart may not be so obvious to us. One aim of Buddhist practice is to achieve a favorable birth in our next life, a goal that can be attained only by restraining from actions that are harmful to others. Therefore, even in the context of such an aim, we find that altruism and a good heart are at the root. It is also very clear that for a bodhisattva to be successful in accomplishing the practice of the six perfections—of generosity, ethical discipline, tolerance, joyous effort, concentration, and wisdom—cooperation with and kindness toward fellow beings are extremely important.

Thus we find that kindness and a good heart form the underlying foundation for our success in this life, our progress on the spiritual path, and our fulfillment of our ultimate aspiration, the attainment of full enlightenment. Hence, compassion and a good heart are not only important at the beginning but also in the middle and at the end. Their necessity and value are not limited to any specific time, place, society, or culture.

Thus, we not only need compassion and human affection to survive, but they are the ultimate sources of success in life. Selfish ways of thinking not only harm others, they prevent the very happiness we ourselves desire. The time has come to think more wisely, hasn't it? This is my belief.

2

Developing Compassion

EFORE WE CAN GENERATE COMPASSION and love, it is important to have a clear understanding of what we understand compassion and love to be. In simple terms, compassion and love can be defined as positive thoughts and feelings that give rise to such essential things in life as hope, courage, determination, and inner strength. In the Buddhist tradition, compassion and love are seen as two aspects of same thing: Compassion is the wish for another being to be free from suffering; love is wanting them to have happiness.

The next matter to be understood is whether it is possible to enhance compassion and love. In other words, is there a means by which these qualities of mind can be increased and anger, hatred, and jealousy reduced? My answer to this is an emphatic, "Yes!" Even if you do not agree with me right now, let yourself be open to the possibility of such development. Let us carry out some experiments together; perhaps we may then find some answers.

For a start, it is possible to divide every kind of happiness and suffering into two main categories: mental and physical. Of the two, it is the mind that exerts the greatest influence on most of us. Unless we are either gravely ill or deprived of basic necessities, our physical condition plays a secondary role in life. If the body is content, we virtually ignore it. The mind, however, registers every event, no matter how small. Hence we should devote our most serious efforts to bringing about mental peace rather than physical comfort.

❦ THE MIND CAN BE CHANGED

From my own limited experience, I am convinced that through constant training we can indeed develop our minds. Our positive attitudes, thoughts, and outlook can be enhanced, and their negative counterparts can be reduced. Even a single moment of consciousness depends on so many factors, and when we change these various factors, the mind also changes. This is a simple truth about the nature of mind.

The thing that we call "mind" is quite peculiar. Sometimes it is very stubborn and very resistant to change. With continuous effort, however, and with conviction based on reason, our minds are sometimes quite honest and flexible. When we truly recognize that there is some need to change, then our minds can change. Wishing and praying alone will not transform your mind; you also need reason— reason ultimately grounded in your own experience. And you won't be able to transform your mind overnight; old habits, especially mental ones, resist quick solutions. But with effort over time and conviction grounded in reason, you can definitely achieve profound changes in your mental attitudes.

As a basis for change, we need to recognize that as long as we live in this world we will encounter problems, things that obstruct the fulfillment of our goals. If, when these happen, we lose hope and become discouraged, we diminish our ability to face these difficulties. If, on the other hand, we remember that not just we but everyone has to undergo suffering, this more realistic perspective will increase our determination and our capacity to overcome troubles. By remembering the suffering of others, by feeling compassion for others, our own suffering becomes manageable. Indeed, with this attitude, each new obstacle can be seen as yet another valuable opportunity to improve our mind, another opportunity for deepening our compassion! With each new experience, we can strive gradually to become more compassionate; that is, we can develop both genuine sympathy for others' suffering and the will to help remove their pain. As a result, our own serenity and inner strength will increase.

❧ How to Develop Compassion

Self-centeredness inhibits our love for others, and we are all afflicted by it to one degree or another. For true happiness to come about, we need a calm mind, and such peace of mind is brought about only by a compassionate attitude. How can we develop this attitude? Obviously, it is not enough for us simply to believe that compassion is important and to think about how nice it is! We need to make a concerted effort to develop it; we must use all the events of our daily life to transform our thoughts and behavior.

First of all, we must be clear about what we mean by *compassion*. Many forms of compassionate feeling are mixed with desire and attachment. For instance, the love parents feel for their child is often strongly associated with their own emotional needs, so it is not fully compassionate. Usually when we are concerned about a close friend, we call this compassion, but it too is usually attachment. Even in marriage, the love between husband and wife—particularly at the beginning, when each partner still may not know the other's deeper character very well—depends more on attachment than genuine love. Marriages that last only a short time do so because they lack compassion; they are produced by emotional attachment based on projection and expectation, and as soon as the projections change, the attachment disappears. Our desire can be so strong that the person to whom we are attached appears flawless, when in fact he or she has many faults. In addition, attachment makes us exaggerate small, positive qualities. When this happens, it indicates that our love is motivated more by personal need than by genuine care for another.

Compassion without attachment is possible. Therefore, we need to clarify the distinctions between compassion and attachment. True compassion is not just an emotional response but a firm commitment founded on reason. Because of this firm foundation, a truly compassionate attitude toward others does not change even if they behave negatively. Genuine compassion is based not on our own projections and expectations, but rather on the needs of the other: irrespective of whether another person is a close friend or an enemy, as long as that person wishes for peace and happiness and wishes to overcome suffering, then on that basis we develop genuine concern for their problem. This is genuine compassion. For a Buddhist practitioner, the goal is to develop this genuine compassion, this genuine wish for the well-being of another, in fact for every living being throughout the universe. Of course, developing this kind of compassion is not at all easy! Let us consider this point more closely.

Whether people are beautiful or plain, friendly or cruel, ultimately they are human beings, just like oneself. Like oneself, they want happiness and do not want suffering. Furthermore, their right to overcome suffering and to be happy is equal to one's own. Now, when you recognize that all beings are equal in both their desire for happiness and their right to obtain it, you automatically feel empathy and closeness for them. Through accustoming your mind to this sense of universal altruism, you develop a feeling of responsibility for others; you wish to help them actively overcome their problems. This wish is not selective; it applies equally to all beings. As long as they experience pleasure and pain just as you do, there is no logical basis to discriminate between them or to alter your concern for them if they behave negatively.

One point I should make here is that some people, especially those who see themselves as very realistic and practical, are sometimes *too* realistic and obsessed with practicality. They may think, "The idea of wishing for the happiness of all beings, of wanting what is best for every single one, is unrealistic and too idealistic. Such an unrealistic idea cannot contribute in any way to transforming the mind or to attaining some kind of mental discipline, because it is completely unachievable."

A more effective approach, they may think, would be to begin with a close circle of people with whom one has direct interaction. Later one can expand and increase the parameters of that circle. They feel there is simply no point in thinking about all beings since there is an infinite number of them. They may conceivably be able to feel some kind of connection with some fellow human beings on this planet, but they feel that the infinite number of beings throughout the universe have nothing to do with their own experience as individuals. They may ask, "What point is there in trying to cultivate the mind that tries to include within its sphere every living being?"

In other contexts, that might be a valid objection. What is important here, however, is to grasp the impact of cultivating such altruistic sentiments. The point is to try to develop the scope of our empathy in such a way that we can extend it to any form of life with the capacity to feel pain and experience happiness. It is a matter of recognizing living organisms as sentient, and therefore subject to pain and capable of happiness.

Such a universal sentiment of compassion is very powerful, and there is no need to be able to identify, in specific terms, with every single living being in order for it to be effective. In this regard it is similar to recognizing the universal nature of impermanence: when we cultivate the recognition that all things and events are impermanent, we do not need to consider individually every single thing that exists in the universe in order to be convinced of it. That is not how the mind works. It is important to appreciate this point.

Given patience and time, it is within our power to develop this kind of universal compassion. Of course our self-centeredness, our distinctive attachment to the feeling of a solid "I," works fundamentally to inhibit our compassion. Indeed, true compassion can be experienced only when this type of self-grasping is eliminated. But this does not mean that we cannot start to cultivate compassion and begin to make progress right away.

❧ How We Can Start

We should begin by removing the greatest hindrances to compassion: anger and hatred. As we all know, these extremely powerful emotions can overwhelm our minds. Nevertheless, despite their power, anger and hatred can be controlled. If we don't control them, these negative emotions will plague us—with no extra effort on their part!—and impede our quest for the happiness of a loving mind.

You may not feel that anger is a hindrance, so, as a start, it is useful to investigate whether anger is of value. Sometimes, when we are discouraged by a difficult situation, anger does seem helpful, appearing to bring with it more energy, confidence, and determination. In these moments, though, we must examine our mental state carefully. While it is true that anger brings extra energy, if we explore the nature of this energy, we discover that it is blind: we cannot be sure whether its result will be positive or negative. This is because anger eclipses the best part of our brain: its rationality. So the energy of anger is almost always unreliable. It can cause an immense amount of destructive, unfortunate behavior. Moreover, if anger increases to the extreme, one becomes a crazy person, acting in ways that are as damaging to oneself as they are to others.

It is possible, however, to develop an equally forceful but far more controlled energy with which to handle difficult situations. This controlled energy comes not only from a compassionate attitude, but also from reason and patience. These are the most powerful antidotes to anger. Unfortunately, many people misjudge reason and patience as signs of weakness. I believe the opposite to be true: that they are the true signs of inner strength. Compassion is by nature gentle, peaceful, and soft, but it is also very powerful. It gives us inner strength and allows us to be patient. It is those who easily lose their patience who are insecure and unstable. Thus, to me, the arousal of anger is usually a direct sign of weakness.

So, when a problem first arises, try to remain humble and maintain a sincere attitude and be concerned that the outcome will be fair. Of course, others may try to take advantage of your concern for fairness, and if your remaining detached only encourages unjust aggression, adopt a strong stand. This should be done with compassion, however, and if it becomes necessary to express your views and take strong countermeasures, do so without anger or ill intent.

You should realize that even though your opponents appear to be harming you, in the end, their destructive activity will damage only themselves. In order to check your own selfish impulse to retaliate, you should recall your desire to practice compassion and assume responsibility for helping prevent the other person from suffering the consequences of their acts. If the measures you employ have been calmly chosen, they will be more effective, more accurate, and more forceful. Retaliation based on the blind energy of anger seldom hits the target.

❧ FRIENDS AND ENEMIES

I must emphasize again that merely thinking that compassion and reason and patience are good will not be enough to develop them. We must wait for difficulties to arise and then attempt to practice them. And who creates such opportunities? Not our friends, of course, but our enemies. They are the ones who give us the most trouble. So if we truly wish to learn, we should consider enemies our best teachers! For a person who cherishes compassion and love, the practice of patience is essential, and for that, enemies are indispensable. So we should feel grateful to our enemies, for it is they who can best help us develop a tranquil mind! Furthermore, it is often the case in both personal and public life that with a change in circumstances, enemies become friends.

Of course, it is natural and right that we all want friends. But is friendship produced through quarrels and anger, jealousy and intense competitiveness? I do not think so. The best way to make friends is to be very compassionate! Only affection brings us genuine close friends. You should take good care of others, be concerned for their welfare, help them, serve them, make more friends, make more smiles. The result? When you yourself need help, you'll find plenty of helpers! If, on the other hand, you neglect the happiness of others, in the long term you will be the loser.

In today's materialistic society, if you have money and power you may seem to have many friends. But they are not friends of yours; they are friends of your money and power. When you lose your wealth and influence, you will find it very difficult to track these people down.

The trouble is that when things in the world go well for us, we become confident that we can manage by ourselves and feel we do not need friends, but as our status or health declines, we quickly realize how wrong we were. So to prepare for that time, to make genuine friends who will help us when the need arises, we ourselves must cultivate compassion!

Though sometimes people laugh when I say it, I myself always want more friends. I love smiles. Because of this I have the problem of knowing how to make more friends and how to get more smiles, in particular, genuine smiles. There are other kinds of smiles, such as sarcastic, artificial, or diplomatic smiles. Many smiles produce no feeling of satisfaction, and sometimes they can even create suspicion or fear, can't they? But a genuine smile really gives us a feeling of freshness and is, I believe, unique to human beings. If these are the smiles we want, then we ourselves must create the reasons for them to appear.

So how do we make friends? Certainly not through hatred and confrontation. It is impossible to make friends by hitting people and fighting with them. A genuine friendship can emerge only through cooperation based on honesty and sincerity, and this means having an open mind and a warm heart. This, I think, is obvious from our own everyday interactions with others.

❧ OVERCOMING THE ENEMY WITHIN

Anger and hatred are our real enemies. They are the forces we most need to confront and defeat, not the temporary "enemies" who appear intermittently throughout our life. And unless we train our minds to reduce their negative force, they will continue to disturb us and disrupt our attempts to develop a calm mind.

To eliminate the destructive potential of anger and hatred entirely, we need to recognize that the root of anger lies in the attitude that cherishes our own welfare and benefit while remaining oblivious to the well-being of others. This self-centered attitude underlies not only anger, but virtually all our states of mind. It is a deluded attitude, mis-perceiving the way things actually are, and this misperception is responsible for all the suffering and dissatisfaction that we experience. Therefore, the first task of a practitioner of compassion and a good heart is to gain an understanding of the destructive nature of this inner enemy and of how it naturally and inevitably leads to undesirable con-sequences.

In order to see this destructive process clearly, we need to become aware of the nature of the mind. I always tell people that the mind is a very complex phenomenon. According to Buddhist philosophy, there are many types of mind, or consciousness, and in Buddhist meditation we develop a deep familiarity with our ever-changing mental states.

In scientific research, we analyze matter in terms of its con-stituent particles. We actualize the potential of the various molecular and chemical compositions and atomic structures that have beneficial value, while we neglect, or in some cases deliberately eliminate, those that lack such useful properties. This discriminatory approach has led to some fascinating results.

If we paid a similar amount of attention to analyzing our mind, the world of experience and mental phenomena, we would discov-er that there are multitudes of mental states, differing in their modes of apprehension, object, degree of intensity of engagement with their object, and so on. Certain aspects of mind are useful and beneficial, so we should correctly identify them and enhance their potential. Like scientists, if we discover upon examination that certain states of mind are unwholesome in that they bring us suffering and problems, then we should seek a way to eradicate them. This is indeed a most worthwhile project. In fact, this is the greatest concern for Buddhist practitioners. It is quite similar to opening one's skull to carry out experiments on those tiny cells with the aim of determining which cells bring us joy and which cells cause disturbances. As long as these inner enemies remain secure within, there is great danger.

When approaching a technique like the Buddhist training of the mind, we must understand and appreciate the complexity of the task we are facing. Buddhist scriptures mention eighty-four thousand types of negative and destructive thoughts, which have eighty-four thousand corresponding approaches or antidotes. It is important not to have the unrealistic expectation that somehow, somewhere, we will find a single magic key that will help us eradicate all of these negativities. We need to apply many different methods over a long period of time in order to bring lasting results. Therefore, we need great determination and patience. It is wrong to expect that once you start Dharma practice, you'll become enlightened within a short period of time, perhaps in one week. This is unrealistic.

The famous Buddhist saint Nagarjuna wrote beautifully about the need for patience and an appreciation for the length of time that is required to really engage in a process of mental training. Nagarjuna said that if—through mental training and discipline, through insight and its skillful application—you can develop within yourself a sense of ease and confidence, an ease that is rooted in a confirmed definitive stance, the time that it takes to become enlightened does not matter. In contrast to Nagarjuna, in our own personal experience, time *does* matter. If we are experiencing an unbearably miserable event, even for a short time, we feel impatient. We want to get out of the state as soon as possible.

Since compassion and a good heart are developed through constant and conscious effort, it is important for us first to identify the favorable conditions that give rise to our own qualities of kindness and then to identify the adverse circumstances that obstruct our cultivation of these positive states of mind. It is therefore important for us to lead a life of constant mindfulness and mental alertness. Our mastery of mindfulness should be such that whenever a new situation arises, we are able to immediately recognize whether the circumstances are favorable or adverse to the development of compassion and a good heart. By pursuing the practice of compassion in such a manner, we will gradually be able to alleviate the effects of the obstructive forces and enhance the conditions that favor the development of compassion and a good heart.

As I mentioned earlier, every kind of happiness and suffering is primarily either physical or mental. When pain comes mainly in the form of physical sensations, it can be alleviated by a positive mental state; if your mental state is calm, this can neutralize the pain. An attitude of acceptance or willingness to endure that physical pain can also make a big difference. On the other hand, if your pain is primarily mental and not physical, then it is very difficult to get any relief from physical comfort. You may attempt to neutralize the pain through sensory gratification, but that never succeeds for long and may in fact make your pain worse. Therefore, it is very useful and important to concentrate on mental training on a daily basis, even apart from spiritual considerations of the time of death or the path to enlightenment. Even for those who are not interested in such long-term concerns, it is more worthwhile to take care of our mind than to only take care of our money.

Of course Buddhism is concerned not only with relieving one's own pain, but with securing the freedom from suffering for all living beings. Yet if it is so difficult to bear our own pain, how can we even conceive of taking on the responsibility for the suffering of all beings? In his great work, *Guide to the Bodhisattva's Way of Life,* the eighth-century Indian master Shantideva says that there is a phenomenological difference between the pain that you experience when you take someone else's pain upon yourself and the pain that comes directly from your own pain and suffering. In the former, there is an element of discomfort because you are sharing the other's pain; however, there is also a certain amount of stability because, in a sense, you are voluntarily accepting that pain. In the voluntary participation in others' suffering there is strength and a sense of confidence. But in the latter case, when you are undergoing your own pain and suffering, there is an element of involuntariness, and because of that lack of control on your part, you feel weak and completely overwhelmed.

In the Buddhist teachings on altruism and compassion, certain expressions are used such as "Disregard your own well-being and cherish the well-being of others." Such exhortations may sound intimidating, but it is important to understand these statements regarding the practice of voluntarily sharing someone else's pain and suffering in their proper context. Fundamentally, the basis on which you can build a sense of caring for others is the capacity to love yourself.

Love for yourself does not arise from some great debt you owe yourself. Rather, the capacity to love yourself is based on the fact that we all naturally desire happiness and want to avoid suffering. And once you recognize this love in relation to yourself, then you can extend it to other sentient beings. Therefore, when you find statements in the teachings such as "Disregard your own well-being and cherish the well-being of others," you should understand them in the context of training yourself according to the ideal of compassion. This

is important if we are not to indulge in self-centered ways of thinking that disregard the impact of our actions on others.

We can develop the attitude of considering other sentient beings
as precious by recognizing the part their kindness plays in our own
experience of joy, happiness, and success. This should be our first
consideration. Next we should consider that, through analysis, we
can see that much of our misery and pain result from a self-centered
attitude that cherishes our own well-being at the expense of others,
whereas much of the joy and sense of security in our lives arise from
thoughts and emotions that cherish the well-being of others. Con-
trasting these two—cherishing ourselves alone versus cherishing others—convinces us of the need to regard others' well-being as precious.

↬ EQUANIMITY

Because genuine compassion is universal and does not discriminate,
cultivating compassion must first involve cultivating equanimity
toward all sentient beings. For example, you may know that such-
and-such a person is your friend or relative in this life, but Buddhism
points out that this person may have been your worst enemy in a
past life. You can apply the same sort of reasoning to someone you
consider an enemy: although this person may behave negatively
toward you and is your enemy in this life, he or she could have been

your best friend or even your mother in a past life. By reflecting upon the fluctuating nature of one's relationships with others and also on the potential that exists in all sentient beings to be both friends and enemies, you can develop this even-mindedness or equanimity.

The practice of developing equanimity involves a form of detachment, but it is important to understand what *detachment* means. Sometimes when people hear about the Buddhist practice of detachment, they think that Buddhism is advocating indifference toward all things, but that is not the case. Cultivating detachment takes the sting out of our emotions toward others that are based on superficial considerations of distance or closeness. Then, on that basis, we can develop a compassion that is truly universal. Detachment does not mean indifference to the world or life—precisely the opposite. A profound experience of detachment is the ground on which we can build genuine compassion extending to all other sentient beings.

3
Global Compassion

BELIEVE that at every level of society—familial, national, and international—the key to a happier and more successful world is the growth of compassion. We do not need to become religious, nor do we need to believe in a particular ideology. All that is necessary is for each of us to develop our good human qualities. I believe that the cultivation of individual happiness can contribute in a profound and effective way to the overall improvement of the entire human community.

We all share an identical need for love, and on the basis of this commonality, it is possible to feel that anybody we meet, in whatever circumstances, is a brother or sister. No matter how new the face or how different the dress or behavior, there is no significant division between us and other people. It is foolish to dwell on external differences because our basic natures are the same.

The benefits of transcending such superficial differences become clear when we look at our global situation. Ultimately humanity is one, and this small planet is our only home. If we are to protect this home of ours, each of us needs to experience a vivid sense of universal altruism and compassion. It is only this feeling that can remove the self-centered motives that cause people to deceive and misuse one another. If you have a sincere and open heart, you naturally feel self-worth and confidence, and there is no need to be fearful of others.

The need for an atmosphere of openness and cooperation at the global level is becoming more urgent. In this modern age, when it comes to dealing with economic situations, there are no longer familial or even national boundaries. From country to country and continent to continent, the world is inextricably interconnected. Each country depends heavily on the others. In order for a country to develop its own economy, it is forced to take seriously into account the economic conditions of other countries as well. In fact, economic improvement in other countries ultimately results in economic improvement in one's own country. In view of these facts about our modern world, we need a total revolution in our thinking and our habits. It is becoming clearer every day that a viable economic system must be based on a true sense of universal responsibility. In other words, what we need is a genuine commitment to the principles of universal brotherhood and sisterhood. This much is clear, isn't it?

This is not just a holy, moral, or religious ideal. Rather, it is the reality of our modern human existence.

If you reflect deeply enough, it becomes obvious that we need more compassion and altruism everywhere. This critical point can be appreciated by observing the current state of affairs in the world, whether in the fields of modern economics and health care, or in political and military situations. In addition to the multitude of social and political crises, the world is also facing an ever-increasing cycle of natural calamities. Year after year, we have witnessed a radical shifting of global climatic patterns that has led to grave consequences: excessive rain in some countries that has brought serious flooding, a shortage of precipitation in other countries that has resulted in devastating droughts. Fortunately, concern for ecology and the environment is rapidly growing everywhere. We are now beginning to appreciate that the question of environmental protection is ultimately a question of our very survival on this planet. As human beings, we must also respect our fellow members of the human family: our neighbors, our friends, and so forth. Compassion, loving-kindness, altruism, and a sense of brotherhood and sisterhood are the keys not only to human development, but to planetary survival.

The success or failure of humanity in the future depends primarily upon the will and determination of the present generation. If we ourselves do not utilize our faculties of will and intelligence, there is no one else who can guarantee our future and that of the next generation. This is an indisputable fact. We cannot place the entire blame on politicians or those people who are seen as directly responsible for various situations; we too must bear some responsibility personally. It is only when the individual accepts personal responsibility that he or she begins to take some initiative. Just shouting and complaining is not good enough. A genuine change must first come from within the individual, then he or she can attempt to make significant contributions to humanity. Altruism is not merely a religious ideal; it is an indispensable requirement for humanity at large.

If we look at human history, we will find that a good heart has been the key in achieving what the world regards as great accomplishments: in the fields of civil rights, social work, political liberation, and religion, for example. A sincere outlook and motivation do not belong exclusively to the sphere of religion; they can be generated by anyone simply by having genuine concern for others, for one's community, for the poor and the needy. In short, they arise from taking a deep interest in and being concerned about the welfare of the larger community, that is, the welfare of others. Actions resulting from this kind of attitude and motivation will go down in history as good, beneficial, and a service to humanity. Today, when we read of such acts from history, although the events are in the past and have become only memories, we still feel happy and comforted because of them. We recall with a deep sense of admiration that this or that person did a great and noble work. We can also see a few examples of such greatness in our own generation.

On the other hand, our history also abounds with stories of individuals perpetrating the most destructive and harmful acts: killing and torturing other people, bringing misery and untold suffering to large numbers of human beings. These incidents can be seen to reflect the darker side of our common human heritage. Such events occur only when there is hatred, anger, jealousy, and unbounded greed. World history is simply the collective record of the effects of the negative and positive thoughts of human beings. This, I think, is quite clear. By reflecting on history, we can see that if we want to have a better and happier future, we must examine our mindset now and reflect on the way of life that this mindset will bring about in the future. The pervasive power of these negative attitudes cannot be overstated.

❧ COMPASSION AND CONFLICT RESOLUTION

Given our current global situation, cooperation is essential, especially in fields such as economics and education. The idea that international differences are paramount has been made less viable by the movement toward a unified Western Europe. This movement is, I think, truly marvelous and very timely. Yet this close work between nations did not come about because of compassion or religious faith, but rather through necessity. There is a growing tendency in the world toward global awareness. Under the current circumstances a closer relationship with others has become an element essential to our very survival. Therefore, the concept of universal responsibility based on compassion and on a sense of brotherhood and sisterhood is now essential. The world is full of conflicts—conflicts due to ideology, religion—even conflicts within families. These are all conflicts based on one person wanting one thing and another wanting something else. But if we try to find the cause of these many conflicts, we discover that there are in fact many different sources, many different causes, even within ourselves.

Yet even before we understand the causes of all our conflicts, we have the potential and ability to come together in harmony. All the causes are relative. Although there are many sources of conflict, there are at the same time many sources of unity and harmony. The time has come to put more emphasis on unity. Here again there must be human affection and patient analysis grounded in compassion.

For example, you may have a different ideological or religious opinion from someone else. If you respect the other's rights and sincerely show a compassionate attitude toward that person, then it does not matter whether their idea is suitable for you; that is secondary. As long as the other person believes in it and derives some benefits from such a viewpoint, it is his or her absolute right. So we must respect that and accept the fact that different viewpoints exist. In the realm of economics as well, one's competitors must also receive some profit, because they too have to survive. When we have a broader perspective based on compassion, I think things become much easier. Once again, compassion is the key factor.

❧ DEMILITARIZATION

In some regards, our world situation today has eased. The Cold War between the former Soviet Union and the United States is over. Instead of looking for new enemies, we should now think and talk seriously about global demilitarization, or at least the idea of demilitarization. I always tell my American friends, "Your strength comes not from nuclear weapons but from your ancestors' noble ideas of freedom, liberty, and democracy."

When I was in the United States in 1991, I had the opportunity of meeting with former President George Bush. At that time we discussed the New World Order, and I said to him, "A New World Order with compassion is very good. I'm not so sure about a New World Order without compassion."

I believe that the time has come to think and talk about demilitarization. With the breakup of the former Soviet Union, we saw some signs of weapons reduction and, for the first time, denuclearization. Step by step, I think our goal should be to free the world—our small planet—from weapons. This does not mean, however, that we should abolish all forms of weapons. We may need to keep some, since there are always some mischievous people and groups among us. In order to take precautions and be safeguarded from these sources, we could create a system of regionally monitored international police forces, not necessarily belonging to any one nation but controlled collectively and supervised ultimately by an organization like the United Nations or a similar international body. That way, with no weapons available to any individual nation, there would be no danger of military conflict between nations, and there would be no civil war.

War, sadly, has remained a part of human history up to the present, but I think the time has come to change the concepts that lead to war. Some people consider war to be something glorious; they think that through war they can become heroes. This attitude toward war is very wrong. Recently an interviewer remarked to me, "Westerners have a great fear of death, but Easterners seem to have very little fear of death."

To that I half-jokingly responded, "It seems to me that, to the Western mind, war and the military establishment are extremely important. War means death—by killing, not by natural causes. So it seems that, in fact, you are the ones who do not fear death, because you are so fond of war. We Easterners, particularly Tibetans, cannot even begin to consider war; we cannot conceive of fighting, because the inevitable result of war is disaster: death, injuries, and misery. Therefore, the concept of war, in our minds, is extremely negative. That would seem to mean we actually have more fear of death than you. Don't you think?"

Unfortunately, because of certain factors, people persist with incorrect ideas about war. The danger of these ideas for the world community is greater than ever, so we need to seriously consider demilitarization. I felt this very strongly during and after the Persian Gulf crisis. Of course, everybody blamed Saddam Hussein, and there is no question that Saddam Hussein was harmful—he made many mistakes and acted wrongly in many ways. After all, he is a dictator, and a dictator is, of course, something harmful. However, without his military establishment, without his weapons, Saddam Hussein could not function as that kind of dictator. Who supplied those weapons? The suppliers also bear the responsibility. Some Western nations supplied him with weapons without regard for the consequences.

To think only of money, of making a profit from selling weapons, is terrible. I once met a Frenchwoman who had spent many years in Beirut. She told me with great sadness that during the crisis in Beirut there were people at one end of the city making a profit selling weapons, and that every day, at the other end of the city, other—innocent—people were being killed with those very weapons. Similarly, on one side of our planet there are people living a lavish life with the profits made from selling arms, while innocent people are getting killed with those sophisticated arms on the other side of our planet. Therefore, the first step is to stop selling weapons. Sometimes I tease my Swedish friends: "Oh, you are really wonderful. During the last period of conflict you remained neutral. And you always consider the importance of human rights and world peace. Very good. But in the meantime you are selling many weapons. This is a little hypocritical, isn't it?"

At the time of the Persian Gulf crisis I made an inner pledge—a commitment that for the rest of my life I would contribute to furthering the idea of demilitarization. As far as my own country is concerned, I have made up my mind that in the future, Tibet should be a completely demilitarized zone. Once again, in working to bring about demilitarization, the key factor is human compassion.

4

Religious Pluralism

NLESS WE KNOW the value of other religious traditions, it is difficult to develop respect for them. Mutual respect is the foundation of genuine harmony. We should strive for a spirit of harmony, not for political or economic reasons, but rather simply because we realize the value of other traditions. I always make an effort to promote religious harmony.

Drawing on religious faith to promote basic human values is something very positive. The major world religions all teach love, compassion, and forgiveness. The way each religious tradition promotes these is different, of course, but since they aim at more or less the same goals—having a happier life, becoming a more compassionate person, and creating a more compassionate world— their different methods do not present an inherent problem. The ultimate achievement of love, compassion, and forgiveness is what is important. All the major world religions have the same potential to help humanity. Some people have a disposition that is suited to religious faith, and because of the variety of dispositions among humans, it logically follows that we need different religions. The variety is beneficial. I'd like to address the topic of religious harmony by defining two levels of spirituality.

✢ THE FIRST LEVEL OF SPIRITUALITY: FAITH AND TOLERANCE

At the first level of spirituality, for human beings everywhere, is faith. This is true for each of the major world religions. I believe each of these religions has its own important role, but in order for them to make an effective contribution to the benefit of humanity, two important factors must be considered.

The first of these factors is that the individual practitioners of the various religions—that is, we ourselves—must practice sincerely. Religious teachings must be an integral part of our lives; they should not be separate from our lives. Sometimes we go into a church or temple and say a prayer or generate some kind of spiritual feeling, and then, when we step outside the church or temple, none of that religious feeling remains. This is not the proper way to practice. The religious message must be with us wherever we are. The teachings of our religion must be present in our lives so that, when we really need or require blessings or inner strength, those teachings and the effects of those teachings will be there for us. They will be there when we experience difficulties because they are constantly present.

Only when religion has become an integral part of our lives can it be really effective. We need to know these teachings not only on an intellectual level but also through our own deeper experience. Sometimes we understand different religious ideas on an overly superficial or intellectual level. Without a deeper feeling, the effectiveness of religion becomes limited. Therefore, we must practice sincerely, and integrate our religion into our lives.

The second factor is concerned more with interaction among the various world religions. Today, because of increasing technological change and the nature of the world economy, we are much more dependent on one another than ever before. Different countries, different continents, have become more closely related to one another. In reality the survival of one region of the world depends on that of others. Therefore, the world has become much closer, much more interdependent. As a result, there is more human interaction on a larger scale. Under such circumstances, the acceptance of pluralism among the world's religions is very important. In previous times, when communities lived separately from one another and religions arose in relative isolation, the idea that there was only one possible religion was very useful. But now the situation has changed, and the circumstances are entirely different. Now, therefore, it is crucial to accept the fact that different religions exist, and in order to develop genuine mutual respect among them, close contact among the various religions is essential. This is the second factor that will enable the world's religions to be effective in benefiting humanity.

When I was in Tibet, I had no contact with people of religious faiths other than Buddhism, so my attitude toward other religions was not very positive. But once I had had the opportunity to meet with people of different faiths and to learn from personal contact and experience, my attitude toward other religions changed. I realized how useful to humanity other religions are, and what potential each has to contribute to a better world. In the last several centuries the various religions have made marvelous contributions toward the betterment of human beings, and even today there are large numbers of followers benefiting from Christianity, Islam, Judaism, Buddhism, Hinduism, and so forth.

To give an example of the value of meeting people of different faiths: My meetings with the late Thomas Merton showed me what a beautiful, wonderful person he was and gave me firsthand insight into the spiritual potential of the Christian faith. On another occasion I met with a Catholic monk in Montserrat, one of Spain's famous monasteries. I was told that this monk had lived for several years as a hermit on a hill just behind the monastery. When I visited the monastery, he came down from his hermitage especially to meet me. As it happened, his English was even worse than mine, and this gave me more courage to speak with him! We remained face to face, and I inquired, "In those years, what were you doing on that hill?"

He looked at me and answered, "Meditation on compassion, on love." As he said those few words, I understood the message through his eyes. I truly developed genuine admiration for this person and for others like him. Such experiences have helped confirm in my mind that all the world's religions have the potential to produce good people, despite their differences of philosophy and doctrine. Each religious tradition has its own wonderful message to convey.

The point here is that for the people who follow those teachings in which the basic faith is in a creator—in God—that approach is very effective for them. Christians, for instance, do not believe in rebirth, and thus do not accept belief in past or future lives. They accept only this life. However, they hold that this very life is created by God, and this idea gives rise in them to a feeling of intimacy with God and dependence on God. What follows from this is the teaching that we should love our fellow human beings. The reasoning is that if we love God, we must love our fellow human beings because they, like us, were created by God. Their future, like ours, depends on the creator; therefore, their situation is like our own. Consequently, the faith of people who tell others to love God but who themselves do not show genuine love toward their fellow human beings is questionable. The person who believes in God and in love for God must demonstrate the sincerity of his or her love of God through love directed toward fellow human beings. This approach is very powerful, isn't it?

Thus, if we examine each religion from various angles in the same way—not simply from our own philosophical position but from several points of view—there can be no doubt that all major religions have the potential to improve human beings. This is obvious. Through close contact with those of other faiths it is possible to develop a broad-minded attitude and mutual respect with regard to other religions. Close contact with different religions helps me to learn new ideas, new practices, and new methods or techniques that I can incorporate into my own practice. Similarly, some of my Christian brothers and sisters have adopted certain Buddhist methods—for example, the practice of one-pointedness of mind as well as techniques to help improve tolerance, compassion, and love. There is great benefit when practitioners of different religions come together for this kind of interchange. In addition to the development of harmony among them, there are other benefits to be gained as well.

Politicians and national leaders frequently talk about coexistence and coming together. Why not we religious people too? I think the time has come. At Assisi, Italy, in 1987, for example, leaders and

is called *interdependent origination:* all things and events, including our experiences of suffering and happiness, arise from the coming together of a multiplicity of causes and conditions.

⚶ Understanding the Primary Role of Mind

If we probe the teaching of the four noble truths carefully, we discover the primary importance that consciousness, or mind, plays in determining our experiences of suffering and happiness. The Buddhist view is that there are different levels of suffering. For example, there is the suffering that is very obvious to all of us, such as painful experiences. This we all can recognize as suffering. A second level of suffering includes what we ordinarily define as pleasurable sensations. In reality, pleasurable sensations are suffering because they have the seed of dissatisfaction within them. There is also a third level of suffering, which in Buddhist terminology is called the pervasive suffering of conditioning. One might say that this third level of suffering is the mere fact of our existence as unenlightened beings who are subject to negative emotions, thoughts, and karmic actions. *Karma* means action and is what keeps us stuck in a negative cycle. Being bound to karma in this way is the third type of suffering.

If you look at these three different kinds of suffering, you will find that all of them are ultimately grounded in states of mind. In fact, undisciplined states of mind in and of themselves are suffering. If we look at the origin of suffering in the Buddhist texts, we find that, although we read about karma and the delusion that motivates karmic action, we are dealing with actions committed by an agent. Because there is always a motive behind every action, karma can also be understood ultimately in terms of a state of mind, an undisciplined state of mind. Similarly, when we talk about delusions that propel one into acting in negative ways, these are also undisciplined states of mind. Therefore, when Buddhists refer to the truth of the origin of suffering, we are talking about a state of mind that is undisciplined and untamed, one that obscures us from enlightenment and causes us to suffer. The origin of suffering, the cause of suffering, and the suffering itself can all be understood ultimately only in terms of a state of mind.

When we talk about the cessation of suffering, we are speaking only in relation to a living being, an agent with consciousness. Buddhist teachings describe cessation of suffering as the highest state of happiness. This happiness should not be understood in terms of pleasurable sensations; we are not talking about happiness at the level of feeling or sensation. Rather, we are referring to the highest level of happiness: total freedom from suffering and delusion. Again, this is a state of mind, a level of realization.

Ultimately, in order to understand our experience of suffering

and pain and the path that leads to cessation—the four noble truths—
we have to understand the nature of mind.

❧ MIND AND NIRVANA

The process by which mind creates the suffering we live in is
described by the Indian master Chandrakirti in his *Guide to the Middle Way* when he states, "An undisciplined state of mind gives rise
to delusions that propel an individual into negative action, which
then creates the negative environment in which the person lives."

To try to understand the nature of freedom from suffering, what
Buddhists call *nirvana,* we can look at a passage in Nagarjuna's
famous *Fundamentals of the Middle Way* where he equates, in some
sense, unenlightened existence *(samsara)* and enlightened existence
(nirvana). The point Nagarjuna makes is that we should not think
there is an intrinsic, essential nature to our existence, be it enlightened or unenlightened. From the point of view of emptiness, they
are equally devoid of any kind of intrinsic reality. That which dif-
ferentiates an unenlightened state from an enlightened state is the
knowledge and the experience of emptiness. The knowledge and
experience of the emptiness of samsara is itself nirvana. The difference between samsara and nirvana is a state of mind.

So, given these premises, it is fair to ask: Is Buddhism suggesting that everything is nothing but a projection of our mind? This is a critical question and one that has elicited different responses from Buddhist teachers throughout the history of Buddhism. In one camp, great masters have argued that in the final analysis everything, including our experience of suffering and happiness, is nothing but a projection of our mind.

But there is another camp that has vehemently argued against this extreme form of subjectivism. This second camp maintains that although one can, in some sense, understand everything, including one's experiences, as creations of one's mind, this does not mean that everything is only the mind. They argue that one must maintain a degree of objectivity and believe that things do in fact exist. Although this camp also maintains that consciousness plays a role in creating our experience and the world, there is at the same time an objective world.

There is another point that I think one should understand with regard to the Buddhist concept of nirvana. Nagabuddhi, a student of Nagarjuna, states that: "Enlightenment or spiritual freedom is not a gift that someone can give to you, nor is the seed for enlightenment something that is owned by someone else." The implication here is that the potential for enlightenment exists naturally in all of us. Nagarjuna's student goes on to ask, "What is nirvana, what is enlighten-

ment, what is spiritual freedom?" He then answers, "True enlightenment is nothing but when the nature of one's own self is fully realized." This nature of one's own self is what Buddhists call the ultimate
clear light, or inner radiant nature of the mind. When this is fully
actualized, or realized, that is enlightenment, that is true buddhahood.

We can see that when we talk about enlightenment and nirvana,
which are fruits of one's spiritual endeavors, we are speaking about
a state of mind. Similarly, when we talk about the delusions that
obstruct our actualization of that enlightened state, we are also talking about states of mind—deluded states of mind. In particular, we are
referring to the delusions that are grounded in a distorted way of perceiving one's own self and the world. The only way we can eliminate
that misunderstanding, that distorted way of perceiving the self and
the world, is through cultivating insight into the true nature of mind.

In summary, the teachings of the Buddha equate, on the one
hand, an undisciplined state of mind with suffering and, on the other
hand, a disciplined state of mind with happiness and spiritual freedom. This is an essential point.

☙ VALID AND INVALID THOUGHT

Mind in Buddhism has a broad meaning that encompasses the whole
spectrum of conscious experience, including all thoughts and emotions.

One natural fact—I suppose one could call it a psychological law—of our subjective experience is that two directly opposing thoughts or emotions cannot coexist at the same time. From our ordinary day-to-day experience, we know that there are thoughts that can be classified as valid and others that are invalid. For example, if a particular thought corresponds to reality, that is, if there is a correspondence between a state of affairs in the world and one's perception of it, then one can call that a valid thought or a valid experience. But we also experience thoughts and emotions that are completely contrary to the way things are. In some cases, they may be forms of exaggeration, but in other cases they may be diametrically opposed to the way things really are. These thoughts and emotions can be called invalid.

Buddhist texts, especially those dealing with ways of knowing, draw on this distinction between valid and invalid thoughts and emotions to discuss valid cognition and its results. The point here is that for an endeavor to be successful and lead to the achievement of an objective, valid thoughts and emotions are required.

In Buddhist texts, the attainment of the highest spiritual liberation is said to be the fruit of valid thoughts and emotions. For example, according to Buddhist teachings, the principal factor that gives rise to enlightenment is said to be true insight into the nature of reality. True insight into the nature of reality is a valid way of knowing things, such as the nature of the world. Compassion, altruism, and *bodhichitta*—the mind of enlightenment—are integral parts of this true insight into reality, and thus, these are all based on valid thought. Although altruism and compassion are more emotions than cognitive thoughts, the process that leads to the realization of universal compassion and bodhichitta involves comparing truths and falsehoods. This is a process of cultivating valid ways of seeing and experiencing things. Therefore, we can say that buddhahood itself is a consequence of valid thoughts and emotions. In contrast, we can see unenlightened experience (samsara) as the product of invalid ways of experiencing.

For example, according to Buddhism, the fundamental root of our unenlightened existence and suffering is ignorance. The primary characteristic of this ignorance is a distorted perception of the world and of ourselves. Once again, invalid thoughts and emotions, invalid ways of seeing and experiencing things and ourselves, are ultimately the source of our suffering and unenlightenment. In the final analysis, valid thoughts and emotions correlate to happiness and spiritual freedom, while invalid thoughts and emotions correlate to suffering and the unenlightened state.

❦ THE TWO TRUTHS

In training the mind, we develop, enhance, and perfect valid thoughts and emotions, and we counteract, undermine, and eventually eliminate invalid forms. The multiple approaches to training the mind have two principal aspects. One is the development of insight or wisdom, that is, developing these valid ways of thinking. The other aspect is method, or *skillful means*. This way of looking at the essence of the teachings of the Buddha as teachings on wisdom and on method corresponds wonderfully to a point Nagarjuna makes. He says that all the teachings of the Buddha must be understood via the two truths, conventional truth and ultimate truth. One has to understand the essential teachings of the four noble truths in terms of these two truths. When we talk about the nature of the two truths, however, we should understand that they are not two independent and unrelated realms.

The various philosophical schools have different understandings of these two truths. When I talk about the two truths, my understanding is grounded on the perspective of the Indian Madhyamika thinkers, toward whom I have a particular bias based on admiration. According to the Madhyamika view, conventional reality is constituted by ordinary experience in the realm of cause and effect. This is the realm of multiplicity where we see the diverse laws of reality at work. This level of reality is called conventional truth because the truth of our experiences at this level is specific to a conventional, or normal, way of understanding the world.

If we probe deeper, we find that each and every thing is the result of many causes and conditions. The origination of things and events is dependent upon multiple factors. What is the implication of this reality of interdependence? It is that no thing or event, including one's own self, possesses an independent or intrinsic reality. This absence of an independent reality is said to be ultimate truth. The reason it is called *ultimate* truth is that it is not obvious to us at our ordinary level of perception of the world. One needs to probe deeper to find it.

These two truths are really two sides of the same thing—two perspectives on one and the same world. The principle of two truths is very important because it directly touches upon our understanding of the relationship between our perception and the reality of the world. We find in the Indian Buddhist literature a tremendous amount of discussion, debate, and analysis concerning how the mind, or consciousness, perceives the world. Questions arise such as: What is the nature of the relationship between our subjective experience and the objective world? and: To what extent are our experiences constituted by the world we perceive? I think the reason there has been such tremendous discussion in Buddhism about these questions is because the answers to them play such a crucial role in the development of one's mind.

❧ THE TWO ASPECTS OF BUDDHAHOOD

Corresponding to these two levels of reality are the two dimensions of the path, method and wisdom. And because there are two principal dimensions to the path there are two aspects to the resultant state of buddhahood. One is the form body of a buddha, and the other is the truth body, the actual reality of an enlightened mind.

The form body is said to be that aspect of a fully enlightened being that exists purely in relation to others. By assuming such diverse forms and appearances, a fully enlightened being can engage in all kinds of activities to ensure the well-being of others. The truth body of a buddha is said to be the aspect that exists in relation to other buddhas. The reason for this is that the truth body is directly accessible only to a fully enlightened being. It is only by assuming a form body that the truth body can manifest and engage in activities that are beneficial to unenlightened beings. So the state of buddhahood can therefore be seen as the fulfillment of both one's own self-interest and the interests of others.

To become a buddha means that one has both fully ascertained the true nature of reality and developed fully the wish to benefit others. A buddha is therefore a complete manifestation of both wisdom and compassion.

6

The Bodhisattva Way

HE *Guide to the Bodhisattva's Way of Life* by the eighth-century Indian master Shantideva is the primary source of most of the literature on the altruistic attitude of putting the happiness of others before our own. I received an oral transmission of this text from the late Khunu Rinpoche, a remarkable teacher from Kinnaur in northern India. I myself try to apply these teachings as much as possible and also, whenever the opportunity arises, explain them to others. Using Shantideva's text as a guide, I would like to explore some of the main points of this compassionate practice.

❧ RECOGNIZING THE ENEMY WITHIN

In order to prioritize the well-being of others, it is first necessary to recognize what keeps us stuck in the self-centered attitude.

Shantideva explains in the fourth chapter, entitled "Conscientious-
ness," that the delusions within our minds, such as hatred, anger,
attachment, and jealousy, are our true enemies. As he states in the
two verses below, these enemies do not have physical bodies with
legs and arms, nor do they hold weapons in their hands; instead, they
reside in our minds and afflict us from within. They control us from
within and bind us to them as their slaves. Normally, however, we do
not realize these delusions as our enemies, and so we never confront
or challenge them. Since we do not challenge them, they reside un-
threatened within our mind and continue to inflict harm on us at will.

> The enemies such as hatred and craving
> Have neither arms nor legs,
> And are neither courageous nor wise;
> How, then, have I been used like a slave by them?
>
> For while they dwell within my mind,
> At their pleasure they cause me harm;
> Yet I patiently endure them without anger.
> But this is an inappropriate and shameful time
>   for patience. (4:28–29)

Negative thoughts and emotions are often deceptive. They play
tricks on us. Desire, for example, appears to us as a trusted friend,

something beautiful and dear to us. Similarly, anger and hatred appear to us like our protectors or reliable bodyguards. Sometimes, when someone is about to harm you, anger rises up like a protector and gives you a kind of strength. Even though you may be physically weaker than your assailant, anger makes you feel strong. It gives you a false sense of power and energy, the result being, in this case, that you might get yourself beaten up. Because anger and other destructive emotions appear in such deceptive guises, we rarely actually challenge them. There are many similar ways in which the negative thoughts and emotions deceive us. In order to fully realize the treachery of these negative thoughts and emotions, we must first achieve some mental stability. Only then will we begin to see their treacherous nature.

Despite being a monk and a supposed practitioner of the *Guide to the Bodhisattva's Way of Life,* I myself still occasionally become irritated and angry and, as a result, use harsh words toward others. Then, a few moments later when the anger has subsided, I feel embarrassed; the negative words are already spoken, and there is truly no way to take them back. Although the words themselves are uttered and the sound of the voice has ceased to exist, their impact lives on. Hence, the only thing I can do is to go to the person and apologize. But in the meantime, I may feel quite shy and embarrassed. This shows that even a short instance of anger and irritation creates a great amount of discomfort and disturbance to the one who gets angry, not to mention the harm caused to the person who is the target of that anger. So in reality, these negative states of mind obscure our intelligence and good judgment and thereby cause great damage.

One of the best human qualities is our intelligence, which enables us to judge what is wholesome and what is unwholesome, what is beneficial and what is harmful. Negative thoughts, such as anger and strong attachment, destroy this special human quality; this is indeed very sad. When anger or attachment dominates the mind, a person becomes almost crazed, and I am certain that nobody wishes to be crazy. Under the power of anger or attachment we commit all kinds of harmful acts—often having far-reaching and destructive consequences. A person gripped by such states of mind and emotion is like a blind person, who cannot see where he is going. Yet we neglect to challenge these negative thoughts and emotions that lead us nearly to insanity. On the contrary, we often nurture and reinforce them! By doing this we are, in fact, making ourselves prey to their destructive power. When you reflect along these lines, you will realize that our true enemy is not outside ourselves.

Let me give you another example. When your mind is trained in self-discipline, even if you are surrounded by hostile forces, your peace of mind will hardly be disturbed. On the other hand, if your mind is undisciplined, your mental peace and calm can easily be disrupted by your own negative thoughts and emotions. So I repeat, the real enemy is within, not outside. Usually we define our enemy as a person, an external agent, whom we believe is causing harm to us or to someone we hold dear. But such an enemy is dependent on many conditions and is impermanent. One moment, the person may act as an enemy; at yet another moment, he or she may become your best friend. This is a truth that we often experience in our own lives. But negative thoughts and emotions, the inner enemy, will always remain the enemy. They are your enemy today, they have been your enemy in the past, and they will remain your enemy in the future as long as they reside within your mind.

This inner enemy is extremely dangerous. The destructive potential of an external enemy is limited when compared to that of its inner counterpart. Moreover, it is often possible to create a physical defense against an external enemy. In the past, for example, even though they had limited material resources and technological capabilities, people defended themselves by building fortresses and castles with many layers of walls. With today's powerfully destructive weapons, such defenses are of course obsolete. In a time when every country is a potential target for the nuclear weapons of others, human beings still continue to develop defense systems of greater and greater sophistication. The missile defense system proposed by the United States is a typical example of such an initiative. Underlying its development is still the old belief that we can eventually create a system that will provide us with the "ultimate" protection. I do not know if it will ever be possible to create a defense system capable of guaranteeing world-wide protection against all external forces of destruction. However, one thing is certain: as long as those destructive internal enemies of anger and hatred are left to themselves unchallenged, the threat of physical annihilation will always loom over us. In fact, the destructive power of an external enemy ultimately derives from the power of these internal forces. The inner enemy is the trigger that unleashes the destructive power of the external enemy. Shantideva tells us that as long as these inner enemies remain secure within, there is great danger.

Shantideva goes on to say that even if everyone in the world were to stand up against you as your enemies and harm you, as long as your own mind was disciplined and calm, they would not be able to disturb your peace. Yet a single instance of delusion arising in your mind has the power to disturb that peace and inner stability.

Should even all the gods and demigods
Rise up against me as my enemies,
They could neither lead nor place me
In the roaring fires of deepest hell.

> But the mighty foe, these disturbing conceptions,
> In a moment, can cast me amidst those flames,
> Which when met will cause not even the ashes
> Of the king of mountains to remain. (4:30–31)

Shantideva also states that one crucial difference between the ordinary enemy and the delusions is that if you relate in a friendly manner and with understanding toward the ordinary enemy, then you might be able to change that enemy into a friend, but you cannot relate to the delusions in a similar way. The more you try to associate with them with the aim of befriending them, the more harmful and disastrous they become.

> If I agreeably honor and entrust myself to others,
> They will bring me benefit and happiness;
> But if I entrust myself to these disturbing conceptions,
> In the future they will bring only misery and harm. (4:33)

As long as you remain under the domination of the delusions and their underlying states of ignorance, you have no possibility of achieving genuine, lasting happiness. This, I think, is a natural fact. If you feel deeply disturbed by this truth, you should respond by seeking a state of freedom from it—that is, the state of nirvana. Those who become monks and nuns take the attainment of nirvana, or true liberation, as the focus of their lives. So if you can afford to devote yourself wholly to the practice of Dharma, then you should implement the spiritual methods in your life that lead to the attainment of this state of freedom. If, as in my own case, you do not have sufficient time, it is quite difficult, isn't it? I know that one factor preventing me from devoting myself fully to such a committed way of life is my own laziness. I am a rather lazy Dalai Lama, the lazy Tenzin Gyatso! Even if you cannot lead a single-minded life of Dharma practice, it is very beneficial to reflect on these teachings as much as possible and make efforts to recognize the transience of all adverse circumstances. Like ripples in a pool, they occur and soon disappear.

Insofar as our lives are conditioned by our past deluded actions, they are characterized by endless cycles of problems, which arise and then subside. One problem appears and passes, and soon another one begins. They come and go in a ceaseless continuum. However, the continuum of each of our consciousnesses—for example, Tenzin Gyatso's consciousness—is beginningless. Though in a state of constant flux, an ever-changing, dynamic process, the basic nature of consciousness never changes. Such is the nature of our conditioned existence, and the realization of this truth makes it easy for me to relate to reality. This realistic outlook helps me maintain my peace and calm. This is the monk Tenzin Gyatso's way of thinking. Through my own experience, I know that the mind can be trained, and by means of that training, we can bring about a profound change within ourselves. That much, I know, is quite certain.

Despite its pervasive influence and destructive potential, there is one particular way in which the inner enemy is weaker than the external enemy. Shantideva explains in the *Guide to the Bodhisattva's Way of Life* that to overcome ordinary enemies you need physical strength and weapons. You might even need to spend billions of dollars on weapons to counter them. But to combat the enemy within, the disturbing conceptions, you need only develop the factors that give rise to the wisdom realizing the ultimate nature of phenomena. You do not need any material weapon nor do you need physical strength. This is very true.

> Deluded disturbing conceptions! If forsaken by the
>   wisdom eye
> And dispelled from my mind, where could you go?
> Where could you dwell in order to be able to injure
>   me again?
> But, weak-minded, I have been reduced to making
>   no effort. (4:46)

Actually, when I was receiving the oral teachings on this text from the late Khunu Rinpoche, I remarked that the *Guide to the Bodhisattva's Way of Life* states that delusions are humble and weak, which is not true. He immediately responded by saying that you do not need an atom bomb to destroy the delusions! So this is what Shantideva means here. You do not need expensive sophisticated weapons to destroy the inner enemy. You simply need to develop a firm determination to defeat them by generating wisdom: a realization of the true nature of the mind. You must also genuinely understand both the relative nature of negative thoughts and emotions as well as the ultimate nature of all phenomena. In technical Buddhist terminology, this insight is known as the *true insight into the nature of emptiness.* Shantideva mentions still another sense in which the inner enemy is weaker. Unlike an external enemy, the inner enemy cannot regroup and launch a comeback once it has been destroyed from within.

❧ OVERCOMING ANGER AND HATRED

We have discussed the deceptive and destructive nature of the delusions. Hatred and anger are the greatest obstacles for a practitioner of bodhichitta, the altruistic wish for enlightenment. Bodhisattvas should never generate hatred, but instead, they should counteract it. For this purpose, the practice of patience, or tolerance, is crucial.

Shantideva begins the sixth chapter of his text, entitled "Patience," by explaining the seriousness of the harm and damage caused by anger and hatred: they harm us now and in the future, and they also harm us by destroying our collection of past merits. Since the practitioner of patience must counteract and overcome hatred, Shantideva emphasizes the importance of first identifying the factors that cause anger and hatred. The principal causes are dissatisfaction and unhappiness. When we are unhappy and dissatisfied, we easily become frustrated and this leads to feelings of hatred and anger.

Shantideva explains that it is very important for those of us training in patience to prevent mental unhappiness from arising—as is prone to occur when you feel that you or your loved ones are threatened, or when misfortune befalls you, or when others obstruct your goals. Your feelings of dissatisfaction and unhappiness on these occasions are the fuel that feeds hatred and anger. So right from the beginning, it is important not to allow such circumstances to disturb your peace of mind.

He emphasizes that we should, with all the means at our disposal, counteract and eliminate the onset of hatred, since its only function is to harm us and others. This is very profound advice.

Having found its fuel of dissatisfaction
In the prevention of what I wish for

And in the doing of what I do not want,

Hatred increases and then destroys me. (6:7)

If maintaining a balanced and happy state of mind even in the face of adversity is a key factor in preventing hatred from arising, we still may wonder how to achieve it. Shantideva says that when you are faced with adverse circumstances, feeling unhappy serves no purpose in overcoming the undesirable situation. It is not only futile but will, in fact, only serve to aggravate your own anxiety and bring about an uncomfortable and dissatisfied state of mind. You lose all sense of composure and happiness. Anxiety and unhappiness gradually eat away inside you and affect your sleep patterns, your appetite, and your health as well. In fact, if the initial harm you experienced was inflicted by an enemy, your mental unhappiness may even become a source of delight for that person. Therefore, it is pointless to feel unhappy and dissatisfied when faced with adverse circumstances or, for that matter, to retaliate against whomever caused you harm.

Generally, there are two types of hatred or anger that result from unhappiness and dissatisfaction. One type is when someone inflicts harm upon you, and as a result you feel unhappy and generate anger. Another type is when, although no person may be directly inflicting harm upon you, as a result of seeing the success and prosperity of your enemies, you feel unhappy and generate anger on that basis.

Similarly, there are generally two types of harm caused by others. One type is direct physical harm inflicted by others and consciously experienced by you. The other type is harm done to your material possessions, reputation, friendship, and so on. Though not directed at your body, these acts are also a type of harm. Let us say that a person hits you with a stick, and you feel pain and become angry. You don't feel angry toward the stick, do you? What exactly is the object of your anger? If it would be appropriate to feel angry toward the factor that impelled the act of hitting, then you should not be angry with the person but with the negative emotions that compelled that person to act. Ordinarily, however, we do not make such distinctions. Instead, we consider the person—the intermediary agent between the negative emotions and the act—as solely responsible, and we hold a grudge against him or her, not against the stick or the delusions.

We should also be aware that since we possess a physical body that is susceptible to pain when hit by a stick, our own body partly contributes to our experience of pain. Because of our body and its nature, we sometimes experience physical pain even when no external causes of pain are present. It is clear then that the experience of pain or suffering comes about as a result of interaction between both our own body and various external factors.

You can also reflect on how, if it is the essential nature of the person who is harming you to inflict harm on others, there is no point in being angry, since there would be nothing that you or that person could do to change their essential nature. If it were truly the person's nature to inflict harm, the person would simply be unable to act otherwise. As stated by Shantideva:

Even if it were the nature of the childish
To cause harm to other beings,
It would still be incorrect to be angry with them.
For this would be like begrudging fire for having
    the nature to burn. (6:39)

On the other hand, if harming is not the person's essential nature, but instead their apparently harmful character is merely incidental and circumstantial, then there is still no need to feel angry toward that person since the problem is entirely due to certain immediate conditions and circumstances. For example, he may have lost his temper and acted badly, even though he did not really mean to hurt you. It is possible to think along these lines as well.

When you feel angry toward others who are not causing you direct, physical harm but whom you perceive as getting in the way of your acquisition of fame, position, material gains, and so forth, you should think in the following manner: Why should I get especially upset or angry about this particular problem? Analyze the nature of what you are being kept from obtaining—fame and so on—and examine carefully their benefit to you. Are they really that important? You will find that they are not. Since that is the case, why be so angry toward that person? Thinking in this way is also useful.

When you become angry as a result of the unhappiness you feel at seeing your enemies' success and prosperity, you should remember that simply being hateful, angry, or unhappy is not going to affect that person's material possessions or success in life. Therefore, even from that point of view, it is quite pointless.

In addition to the practice of patience, those practitioners who take Shantideva's text as inspiration are also seeking to develop bodhichitta—the wish to achieve enlightenment for the benefit of all sentient beings—as well as compassion and mind training. If, despite their practice, they still feel unhappy about their enemies' success in life, then they should remember that this attitude is very inappropriate for a practitioner of compassion. If this negative attitude persists, the thought "I am a practitioner of compassion; I am someone who lives according to the precepts of mind training" becomes mere words devoid of meaning. Instead, a true practitioner of bodhichitta should rejoice that others have been able to achieve something on their own without one's help. Rather than being unhappy and hateful, we should rejoice in the success of others.

If we investigate on a still deeper level, we will find that when enemies inflict harm on us, we can actually feel gratitude toward them. Such situations provide us with rare opportunities to put to test our own practice of patience. It is a precious occasion to practice not only patience but the other bodhisattva ideals as well. As a result, we have the opportunity to accumulate merit in these situations and to receive the benefits thereof. The poor enemy, on the other hand, because of the negative action of inflicting harm on someone out of anger and hatred, must eventually face the negative consequences of his or her own actions. It is almost as if the perpetrators of the harm sacrifice themselves for the sake of our benefit. Since the merit accumulated from the practice of patience was possible only because of the opportunity provided us by our enemy, strictly speaking, we should dedicate our merit to the benefit of that enemy. This is why the *Guide to the Bodhisattva's Way of Life* speaks of the kindness of the enemy.

Although we might recognize, on the one hand, the kindness of the enemy, we might feel, on the other, that the enemy had no intention to be kind to us. Therefore, we think, it is not necessary for us to remember his or her kindness at all. If, in order to respect or hold something dear, there must be conscious intent from the side of the object, then this argument should apply equally to other subjects as well. For example, from their sides, the true cessation of suffering and the true path leading to cessation—the third and fourth noble truths—have no conscious intention to be beneficial. Yet as Buddhists we still respect and revere them. Why? Because we derive benefit from them. If the benefits we derive justify our reverence and respect for these two truths, despite their not having any conscious intention, then this same rationale should apply to the enemy as well.

However, you might feel that there is a major difference between the enemy and these two truths of true cessation and true path. Unlike the two truths, the enemy has a conscious will to harm you. But this difference is also not a valid reason not to respect the enemy. In fact, if anything, it is additional grounds to revere and be grateful to your enemy. It is indeed this special factor that makes your enemy unique. If the mere inflicting of physical pain were sufficient to make someone an enemy, you would have to consider your doctor an enemy, for he often causes pain during treatment. Now, as a genuine practitioner of compassion and bodhichitta, you must develop patience. And in order to practice sincerely and to develop patience, you need someone who willfully hurts you. Thus, these people give us real opportunities to practice these things. They are testing our inner strength in a way that even our guru cannot. Even the Buddha possesses no such potential. Therefore, the enemy is *the only one* who gives us this golden opportunity. That is a remarkable conclusion, isn't it! By thinking along these lines and using these reasons, you will eventually develop a kind of extraordinary respect toward your enemies. This is Shantideva's primary message in the sixth chapter.

Once you generate genuine respect toward your enemy, you can then easily remove most of the major obstacles to developing infinite altruism. Shantideva mentions that, just as the many buddhas help us achieve enlightenment, there is an equal contribution from ordinary sentient beings as well. Enlightenment can only be achieved in reliance upon both of these: the kindness of sentient beings, and the kindness of the buddhas.

For those of us who claim to be followers of Buddha Shakyamuni and who revere and respect the bodhisattva ideals, Shantideva states that it is incorrect to hold grudges or have hatred toward our enemies, when all the buddhas and bodhisattvas hold all sentient beings dear to their hearts. Of course, our enemies are included within the field of all sentient beings. If we hold grudges toward those whom the buddhas and bodhisattvas hold close to their hearts, we contradict the ideals and experience of the buddhas and bodhisattvas, those very beings whom we are trying to emulate.

Even in worldly terms, the more respect and affection we feel toward people, the more consideration we have for them. We try to avoid acting in ways that they might disapprove of, thinking that we might offend them. We try to take into consideration our friends' ways of thinking, their principles, and so on. If we do this even for our ordinary friends, then, as practitioners of the bodhisattva ideals, we should show the same, if not higher, regard for the buddhas and bodhisattvas by trying to not hold grudges and hateful feelings toward our enemies.

Shantideva concludes this chapter on patience by explaining the benefits of practicing patience. In summary, through practicing patience, not only will you reach a state of omniscience in the future, but even in your everyday life you will experience its practical benefits. You will be able to maintain your peace of mind and live a joyful life.

When we practice patience to overcome hatred and anger, it is important to be equipped with the force of joyous effort. We should be skillful in cultivating joyous effort. Shantideva explains that, just as we must be mindful when undertaking a mundane task, such as waging war, to inflict the greatest possible destruction on the enemy while at the same time protecting ourselves from the enemy's harm, in the same way, when we undertake the practice of joyous effort, it is important to attain the greatest level of success while assuring that this action does not damage or hinder our other practices.

❧ ONESELF AND OTHERS: EXCHANGING PLACES

In the chapter on meditation in the *Guide to the Bodhisattva's Way of Life*, we find an explanation of the actual meditation for cultivating compassion and bodhichitta. The explanation follows a method called *equalizing and exchanging oneself and others*. Equalizing and exchanging oneself and others means developing the attitude that understands that, "Just as I desire happiness and wish to avoid suffering, the same is true of all other living beings, who are infinite as space; they too desire happiness and wish to avoid suffering." Just as we work for our own benefit in order to gain happiness and protect ourselves from suffering, we should also work for the benefit of others, to help them attain happiness and freedom from suffering.

Although there are different parts to our body, such as our head, limbs, and so on, insofar as the need to protect them is concerned, there is no difference among them, for they are all equally parts of the same body. In the same manner, all sentient beings have this natural tendency—wishing to attain happiness and be free from suffering—and, insofar as that natural inclination is concerned, there is no difference whatsoever between sentient beings. Consequently, we should not discriminate between ourselves and others as we work to gain happiness and overcome suffering.

We should reflect upon and make serious efforts to dissolve our view that we and others are separate and distinct. We have seen that insofar as the wish to gain happiness and to avoid suffering is concerned, there is no difference at all. The same is also true of our *natural right* to be happy; just as we have the right to enjoy happiness and freedom from suffering, all other living beings have the same natural right. So wherein lies the difference? The difference lies in the number of sentient beings involved. When we speak of the welfare of ourselves, we are speaking of the welfare of only one individual, whereas the welfare of others encompasses the well-being of an infinite number of beings. From that point of view, we can understand that others' welfare is much more important than our own.

If our own and others' welfare were totally unrelated and independent of one another, we could make a case for neglecting others' welfare. But that is not the case. I am always related to others and heavily dependent on them, no matter what my level of spiritual development: while I am unenlightened, while I am on the path, and also once I have achieved enlightenment. If we reflect along these lines, the importance of working for the benefit of others becomes naturally apparent.

You should also examine whether, by remaining selfish and self-centered despite the above points, you can still achieve happiness and fulfill your desires. If you could do so, then pursuit of your selfish and self-centered habits would be a reasonable course of action. But it is not. The nature of our existence is such that we must depend on the cooperation and kindness of others for our survival. It is an observable fact that the more we take the welfare of others to heart and work for their benefit, the more benefit we attain for ourselves.

You can see this fact for yourself. On the other hand, the more self-ish and self-centered you remain, the more lonely and miserable you become. You can also observe this fact yourself.

Therefore, if you definitely want to work for your own benefit and welfare, then it is better to take into account the welfare of others and to regard their welfare as more important than your own. By contemplating these points, you will certainly be able to strengthen more and more your attitude of cherishing the well-being of others.

Furthermore, we can complement our practice of compassion and bodhichitta with meditations on the various factors of wisdom. For example, we can reflect upon buddha-nature: the potential to actualize buddhahood that resides within ourselves and all sentient beings. We can also reflect on the ultimate nature of phenomena, their empty nature, by using logical reasoning to ascertain the nature of reality. We can reflect that the cessation of suffering is possible because the ignorance that is its root cause is by nature adventitious and, hence, can be separated from the essentially pure nature of our mind. By thinking and meditating on the factors of wisdom and maintaining a sustained practice of compassion and altruism with concerted effort over a long period of time, you will see a real change in your mind.

7

Eight Verses for Training the Mind

ALL THE DIVERSE TEACHINGS of the Buddha provide methods for training and transforming the mind. Historically, however, a traditional class of practices and the literature associated with them developed in Tibet known as *lojong,* which means "mind training." These practices are so called because they aim at nothing short of bringing about a radical transformation in our thinking and, through it, helping us to live a compassionate life. One of the principal characteristics of lojong practice is the emphasis it places on overcoming our deluded grasping at a solid ego and the self-cherishing attitudes based on this misapprehension of self. The self-cherishing attitude obstructs our generation of genuine empathy toward others and limits our outlook to the narrow confines of our own self-centered concerns. In essence, with mind training, we seek to transform our normal selfish outlook on life into a more altruistic one, which, at the very least, regards the welfare of others as equal in importance to our own, and ideally regards others' welfare as much more important than ours.

One particularly important piece of mind-training literature is *Eight Verses for Training the Mind* by the twelfth-century master Langri Tangpa. *Eight Verses for Training the Mind* summarizes the key teachings on both wisdom and method. It focuses on the antidotes that enable the practitioner to counter the two principal obstacles. The first obstacle is the self-cherishing attitude, and the antidotes for this are chiefly the cultivation of altruism, compassion, and bodhichitta. The second obstacle is our deluded grasping at some kind of enduring, permanently existing self. The antidote to this is contained in the wisdom teachings. The first seven verses of *Eight Verses for Training the Mind* deal with the practices associated with cultivating method, and the eighth verse deals with the practices for cultivating wisdom. These eight verses can therefore be said to contain the entire essence of the Buddha's teachings in a distinct form.

1   By thinking of all sentient beings
    as even better than the wish-granting gem
    for accomplishing the highest aim,
    may I always consider them precious.

These four lines are about cultivating a sense of holding dear all other sentient beings. The main point this verse emphasizes is to develop an attitude that enables you to regard other sentient beings as precious, much as we might regard precious jewels.

In this verse, there is an explicit reference to the agent "I": "May *I* always consider others precious." Perhaps a brief discussion on the Buddhist understanding of what this "I" is referring to might be helpful.

Generally speaking, no one disputes that people—you, me, others—exist. We do not question the existence of someone who undergoes the experience of pain, for example. We say, "I see such-and-such" and "I hear such-and-such," and we constantly use the first-person pronoun in our speech. There is no disputing the existence of the conventional level of "self" that we all experience in our day-to-day life.

Questions arise, however, when we try to understand what that "self" or "I" really is. In probing these questions we may try to extend the analysis beyond day-to-day life—we may, for example, recollect ourselves in our youth. When you recollect something from your youth, you have a close sense of identification with the state of the body and your sense of self at that age. When you were young, there was a self. As you get older there is a self. There is also a self that pervades both stages. An individual can recollect his or her experiences of youth, his or her experiences of old age, and so on. We identify with our bodily states and sense of self, our "I" consciousness.

Many philosophers and, particularly, religious thinkers have sought to understand the nature of the individual, that "self" or "I," that maintains this continuity over time. This has been especially important within the Indian tradition. The non-Buddhist Indian schools talk about *atman,* which is roughly translated as "self" or "soul"; and in other non-Indian religious traditions, such as Christianity and Judaism, we hear discussion about the "soul" of a being.

In the Indian context, *atman* has the distinct meaning of an agent that is independent of the living and breathing individual. In the Hindu tradition, for example, there is a belief in reincarnation, which has inspired a lot of debate. I have also found references to certain forms of mystical practice in which a consciousness or soul assumes the body of a newly dead person. In order to make sense of a soul assuming another body, we would need to posit some kind of agent that is independent of the observable elements of the individual. On the whole, non-Buddhist Indian schools have more or less come to the conclusion that *self* refers to this independent agent, to something that is independent of our body and mind. Buddhist traditions, on the other hand, have rejected the temptation to posit a "self," an atman, or a soul that is independent of our body and mind.

Among Buddhist schools the consensus is that "self" or "I" must be understood solely in terms of the body and mind. But as to what, exactly, we refer when we say "I" or "self," there has been divergence of opinion even among Buddhist thinkers. Many Buddhist schools maintain that in the final analysis we must identify the self with the consciousness of the person. Through analysis, we can show how our body is a kind of contingent fact, and that what continues across time is really a being's consciousness.

Of course, other Buddhist thinkers have rejected the move to identify self with consciousness, resisting the urge to seek some kind of eternal, abiding, or enduring self. Such thinkers have argued that following that kind of reasoning is, in a sense, succumbing to the ingrained need to grasp at something. An analysis of the nature of self along these lines will yield nothing, because the quest involved here is not scientific but metaphysical; for in the quest for a metaphysical self, we are going beyond the domain of everyday language and everyday experience. Therefore "self," "person," and "agent" must be understood purely in terms of how we experience our sense of self. We should not go beyond the level of the conventional understanding of self and person. We should develop an understanding of our existence in terms of our bodily and mental existence so that "self" and "person" are in some sense understood as designations wholly dependent upon mind and body.

Chandrakirti used the example of a chariot in his *Guide to the*

Middle Way. When you subject the concept of *chariot* to analysis, you are never going to find some kind of metaphysically or substantially real chariot that is independent of the parts of the chariot. But this does not mean the chariot doesn't exist. Similarly, when we subject "self" to such analysis, we cannot find a self independent of the mind and body that constitutes the existence of the individual.

This understanding of the self as arising interdependently must also extend to our understanding of other sentient beings. We designate "sentient beings" in dependence upon their constituent body and mind, what Buddhists call their *aggregates*.

> 2   Wherever I go, with whomever I go,
>   may I see myself as lower than all others, and
>   from the depth of my heart
>   may I consider them supremely precious.

The first verse pointed to the need to cultivate the thought of regarding all other sentient beings as precious. In the second verse, the point being made is that the recognition of the preciousness of other sentient beings, and the sense of caring that you develop on that basis, should not be grounded on a feeling of pity toward other sentient beings, that is, on the thought that they are inferior. Rather, what is being emphasized is a sense of caring for other sentient beings and a recognition of their preciousness, based on reverence and respect, as superior to us.

Moving on to another line of the verse, I think it is important to understand the expression "May I see myself as lower than all others" in the right context. Certainly it is not saying that you should engage in thoughts that would lead to lower self-esteem, or that you should lose all sense of hope and feel dejected, thinking, "I'm the lowest of all. I have no capacity, I cannot do anything and have no power." This is not the kind of consideration of lowness that is being referred to here.

Regarding oneself as lower than others has to be understood in relative terms. In certain ways, human beings can be regarded as superior to animals. We are equipped with the ability to judge between right and wrong and to think about the future. However, you could also argue that in other respects human beings are inferior to animals. For example, animals might not have the ability to judge between right and wrong in a moral sense, and they might not have the ability to see the long-term consequences of their actions, but within the animal realm there is a certain sense of order. If you look at the African savanna, you will see that predators prey on other animals only out of necessity when they are hungry. When they are not hungry, you can see them coexisting quite peacefully. But we human beings, despite our ability to judge between right and wrong, sometimes act out of pure greed. Sometimes we engage in actions purely out of indulgence—we kill out of a sense of sport, say, when we go hunting or fishing. So, in a sense, one could argue that human beings have proven to be *inferior* to animals. It is in such relative terms that we can regard ourselves as lower than others.

One of the reasons for using the word *lower* is to emphasize that normally when we give in to ordinary emotions of anger, hatred, strong attachment, and greed, we do so without any sense of restraint. Often we are totally oblivious to the impact our behavior has on other sentient beings. But by deliberately cultivating the thought of regarding others as superior and worthy of reverence, you provide yourself with a basis for restraint. Then, when emotions arise, they will not be so powerful that they can cause you to disregard the impact of your actions upon others. It is on these grounds that recognizing others as superior to yourself is suggested.

3   May I examine my mind in all actions
    and as soon as a negative state occurs,
    since it endangers myself and others,
    may I firmly face and avert it.

This verse gets to the heart of what could be called the essence of the practice of the Buddhadharma. When we talk about Dharma in the context of Buddhism, we are talking about the cessation of suffering, or nirvana—the true Dharma. There are many levels of cessation; for example, restraint from murder could be Dharma. But this cannot be called Buddhist Dharma specifically because restraint from killing is something that even someone who is nonreligious can adopt as a result of obeying the law.

The essence of the Dharma in the Buddhist tradition is the state of freedom from suffering and from the defilements that lie at the root of suffering. This verse addresses how to combat these defilements, these afflictive emotions and thoughts. For a Buddhist practitioner, the real enemy is this enemy within. It is these emotional and mental afflictions that give rise to pain and suffering. The real task of a practitioner of Buddhadharma is to defeat this inner enemy.

Since applying antidotes to these mental and emotional defilements lies at the heart of Dharma practice and is in some sense its foundation, the third verse suggests that it is very important to cultivate mindfulness right from the beginning. If you let negative emotions and thoughts arise inside you without any restraint, without any mindfulness of their negativity, then you are giving them free rein, and they can then develop to the point where there is no way to counter them. However, if you develop mindfulness of their negativity, then when they occur you will be able to stamp them out as soon as they arise. You will not give them the opportunity or the space to develop into full-blown negative emotional thoughts.

The verse suggests that we apply an antidote at the level of the felt experience. Instead of getting at the root of all emotion, the text suggests antidotes to specific negative emotions and thoughts. For example, to counter anger, you should cultivate love and compassion. To counter strong attachment to an object, you should cultivate thoughts about the impurity of that object, its undesirable nature, and so on. To counter your arrogance or pride, you need to reflect upon your shortcomings in order to give rise to a sense of humility. You can, for example, think about all the things in the world about which you are completely ignorant. Take sign language interpreters for the deaf: when I look at them and see the complex gestures with which they perform translations, I haven't a clue what is going on, and to see that is quite a humbling experience. From my own personal experience, whenever I have a little tingling sense of pride, I think of computers. It really calms me down!

> 4 When I see beings of a negative disposition
> or those oppressed by negativity or pain,
> may I, as if finding a treasure, consider them precious
> for they are rarely met.

The reason beings of negative disposition are identified separately as a focus of training one's mind is because when you encounter such people, you may give in to the temptation to react in some strong negative way. In a sense, such beings pose a greater challenge to your ability to maintain your basic training, and hence they merit our special attention.

You can then go on to apply this sentiment to society in general. Among ordinary people there is a temptation or tendency to reject certain groups of people, to marginalize them and to not want to embrace them within the wider fold of the community. People who are branded as criminals are an example. In these cases, it is even more important for the practitioner to make an extra effort to try to embrace them so that they may be given a second chance in society and also an opportunity to restore their sense of self-esteem. Similarly, there is also within society the temptation to ignore or deny the existence of incurable illnesses, such as AIDS, when one thinks, "That will never happen to me." There is a tendency to turn a blind eye to these things. In these cases too, a true practitioner should consciously reflect upon such phenomena and try to face them. One should cultivate one's mind so that one can empathize and relate to them.

5   Whenever others, out of jealousy,
     revile and treat me in other unjust ways,
     may I accept this defeat myself
     and offer the victory to others.

From a conventional legal point of view, if allegations are made against someone unjustly with no grounds or basis, we feel justified in reacting with anger and a sense of injustice. For a Buddhist practitioner, however, it is recommended that you not react this way, especially if the consequence of that unjust treatment is that you alone and no one else is hurt. A true practitioner of mind training is encouraged to accept defeat and offer victory, averting an outburst of outrage and anger.

> 6   When someone whom I have helped
>   or in whom I have placed great hope
>   harms me with great injustice,
>   may I see that one as a sacred friend.

Usually when we help someone, we tend to expect something in return. When someone is close to us, we have certain expectations of that person. And if that person, instead of responding to us in a positive way and repaying our kindness, inflicts harm upon us, we normally feel a sense of outrage. Our sense of disappointment and hurt are so strong and so deep that we feel that we are entirely justified in reacting with outrage and anger. For a true practitioner it is suggested that you not give in to that kind of normal response but rather utilize the opportunity for training, as a lesson and a teaching. The practitioner should regard that person as a true teacher of patience, for it is in situations like this that the training of patience is most needed. One should acknowledge the value of that person as a rare, precious teacher instead of reacting with anger and hostility.

This is not to suggest, however, that a true practitioner should simply yield to whatever harm or injustice is being inflicted upon him or her. In fact, according to the precepts of the bodhisattva, one should respond to injustice with a strong countermeasure, especially if there is any danger that the perpetrator of the crime is going to continue negative actions in the future or if other sentient beings are adversely affected. What is required is sensitivity to context. If a particular injustice happens and brings no wider consequences to bear upon either the perpetrator of the crime or upon other sentient beings, then perhaps you should let it pass.

7   In short, may I offer both directly and indirectly
    all joy and benefit to all beings, my mothers,
    and may I myself
    secretly take on all of their hurt and suffering.

In this verse the compassion referred to is so strong that, at least at the level of thought, one is willing take upon oneself all the suffering, pain, and hurt of all beings and to take on the negativities that lie at the root of these sufferings. One can also share all the positive qualities one has, such as one's joy, the causes of joy, roots of virtue, positive actions, and so on. One offers these positive qualities to other sentient beings.

The adverb *secretly* refers to the *tonglen* practice, the practice of giving and taking—taking on the suffering of others and offering them our joy and virtue. As the word *secretly* suggests, it is a form of practice that may not be suitable at the beginning stage, for it requires a certain depth of courage and commitment. In terms of the actual practice of giving and taking, tonglen practice is done in conjunction with the process of breathing—exhaling and inhaling.

The word *secretly* may also indicate the need for integrity on the part of the practitioner so that the practice of tonglen is done in a discreet way and the practitioner does not become an exhibitionist. A true practitioner must cultivate a spiritual training such as tonglen discreetly. The Kadampa master Geshe Chekawa states in his *Seven-Point Training of the Mind,* "Our inner states of mind and thoughts and emotions need to be radically transformed and overhauled, but our external appearance should remain the same." The point here is that it is dangerous for practitioners to succumb to the temptation to show off. Sometimes what happens, especially these days, is that people who have only a little experience may assume an air of importance or spirituality, which only cheapens one's true experience. Genuine practice of mind training requires humility and integrity.

The reference to all beings here as "my mothers" suggests the practice of holding all beings to be as dear as our own mother. In the Buddhist teachings on rebirth, in fact, all beings are said to have been our mother in a past life—giving birth to us, feeding us, and keeping us from harm—and we should recall that kindness, even when someone currently appears to us as harmful.

8 May they not be defiled by the concepts
    of the eight mundane concerns
    and, aware that all things are illusory,
    may they, ungrasping, be free from bondage.

The first two lines of this verse emphasize the need to ensure that spiritual practice and mind training are not polluted by worldly concerns such as fame, wealth, and pleasure. This is important even for a spiritual teacher. For example, when I sit on the throne and give a lecture, if somewhere in my thoughts there is a sense of curiosity— "Have I performed well?" "What do people think of my lecture?" "Are they happy with it?" "Will they praise me?"—this will pollute the spiritual training. These mundane concerns should not obscure and pollute true spiritual training.

The last two lines of this verse stress the need to situate mind training within a full understanding of ultimate truth, of emptiness. These lines state that you should develop the awareness that all things are illusory and, without grasping, free yourself from bondage. But before you can understand everything in terms of its illusory nature, you first need to negate the substantial reality of everything, including your own "self." There is no possibility of perceiving the illusory nature of everything unless you first negate the substantial reality of existence.

How do we develop this understanding? It is not enough simply to imagine that everything is empty and devoid of substantial existence or to simply repeat this verse in one's mind, like a formula. What is required is a genuine insight into emptiness through a rational process of analysis and reflection.

One of the most effective and convincing ways to understand how everything lacks a substantial reality is to understand interdependence, the dependent origination of everything. What is unique about the understanding of dependent origination is that it provides us with the possibility of finding that middle way between total nothingness on the one hand and substantial or independent existence on the other. The understanding that things are interdependent and dependently originated in itself suggests that things lack independent existence. And the idea that things originate in relation to others through a complex matrix of dependently originating elements also protects you from the danger of falling into the opposite view of nihilism—thinking that nothing exists. So by finding that true middle way, you can arrive at a genuine understanding and insight into emptiness.

Once you find this kind of insight in your meditation, when you interact with the world, with the people and objects around you, there is a new quality to your engagement with the world that arises out of your awareness of the illusory nature of reality. This new way of engaging in the world gives us a certain freedom from narrow concerns and allows us to work more steadily for the well-being of others. As such, it is a powerful basis for living the compassionate life.

APPENDIX

Generating the Mind of Enlightenment

E HAVE SPOKEN about the nature of compassion and the procedure for training one's mind and cultivating compassion. The special verses below are recited for the purpose of generating bodhichitta, the wish to free all sentient beings from suffering. When reciting the verses, you should try to recollect your full understanding of compassion and the need for cultivating it.

The first verse is a formal taking of refuge. Those of you who are practicing Buddhists, take refuge here. Non-Buddhist religious practitioners—Christians, Jews, Muslims, and others—can take refuge in your own religion's deity and use that formula as a way of reaffirming your faith in that deity.

The second verse pertains to the generation of the mind of enlightenment. The third verse really gives us a sense of courage and also a sense of inspiration that help us sustain our commitment to the altruistic principles. As you recite these verses, you should reflect upon their meaning and cultivate the right contemplation in your mind.

I think these three verses are very powerful. If you agree and feel comfortable with them, you should think about and recite these verses whenever you have the time. It will give you some inner strength, and this is very valuable.

> With a wish to free all beings
> I shall always go for refuge
> to the Buddha, Dharma, and Sangha,
> until I reach full enlightenment.

> Enthused by wisdom and compassion
> today in the Buddha's presence
> I generate the mind for full awakening
> for the benefit of all sentient beings.

> As long as space remains,
> as long as sentient beings remain,
> until then, may I too remain
> and dispel the miseries of the world.

Index

Suggested Further Reading

By the Dalai Lama

THE GOOD HEART

A Buddhist Perspective on the Teachings of Jesus

224 pages, 0-86171-138-6, $14.95

"Arguably the best book on inter-religious dialogue published to date. One does not say such things lightly, but in a very real sense this is a holy book."—Huston Smith, author of *The Illustrated World's Religions*

THE WORLD OF TIBETAN BUDDHISM

An Overview of Its Philosophy and Practice

Translated and edited by Geshe Thupten Jinpa

224 pages, 0-86171-097-5, $15.95

"The definitive book on Tibetan Buddhism by the World's ultimate authority."—*The Reader's Review*

"The perfect introduction for Westerners."—*Small Press*

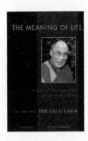

THE MEANING OF LIFE

Buddhist Perspectives on Cause and Effect

164 pages, 0-86171-173-4, $15.95

"The Dalai Lama's kindness and wit make this journey into the inner psychic environment highly accessible. His Holiness presents the basic world view of Buddhism while answering some of life's most profound and challenging questions."—*Branches of Light*

"The Dalai Lama's responses to questions convey a sense of his personal warmth and compassion."—*CHOICE*

"Studded with jewels."—*Shambhala Sun*

IMAGINE ALL THE PEOPLE

The Dalai Lama with Fabien Ouaki

192 pages, 0-86171-150-5, $14.95

If you could sit down with the Dalai Lama and talk about anything, what would you discuss? Here, in spontaneous, lively discussion, the Dalai Lama holds forth on money, politics, and life as it could be.

MINDSCIENCE

An East-West Dialogue

The Dalai Lama and others.

152 pages, 0-86171-066-5, $14.95

Robert A.F. Thurman, Daniel Goleman, and authorities from the fields of psychiatry, psychology, neuroscience, and education join His Holiness for an explorative, historic dialogue between modern science and Buddhism.

"Slender but comprehensive...cuts right to the core issues of its compelling topic."—*The Quest*

"Lively and interesting...full of pearls."—*Shambhala Sun*

KALACHAKRA TANTRA

Rite of Initiation

Translated by Jeffrey Hopkins

512 pages, 0-86171-151-3, $22.95

Of the hundreds of tantras, Kalachakra is the among the most important. Here, the Dalai Lama presents the series of initiations for the generation stage of this tantra, interspersed with his commentary. Eminent scholar Jeffrey Hopkins provides a comprehensive introduction to the symbolism and history behind the practice.

OPENING THE EYE OF NEW AWARENESS

160 pages, 0-86171-155-6, $14.95

"All of His Holiness' many publications are in some sense commentaries on this first book. A clear and concise exposition of the essentials of Buddhist thought."—from the Introduction by Donald Lopez, Jr.

SLEEPING, DREAMING, AND DYING

An Exploration of Consciousness

264 pages, 0-86171-123-8, $16.95

"Intelligent, insightful. Anyone interested in psychology, neuroscience, or the alternative worlds of dreams and the afterlife will surely enjoy the discoveries contained within."—*NAPRA ReView*

WISDOM PUBLICATIONS
Publisher of Buddhist Books. For everyone.
199 Elm Street, Somerville, MA 02144 USA
wisdompubs.org ∼ 800.272.4050

Distributed to the trade by: National Book Network (NBN)
Ph: 800.462.6420 ∼ Fax: 800.338.4550

About Wisdom

Wisdom Publications, a not-for-profit publisher, is dedicated to making available authentic Buddhist works for the benefit of all. We publish translations of the sutras and tantras, commentaries and teachings of past and contemporary Buddhist masters, and original works by the world's leading Buddhist scholars. We publish our titles with the appreciation of Buddhism as a living philosophy and with the special commitment to preserve and transmit important works from all the major Buddhist traditions.

If you would like to learn more about Wisdom, or to browse our books online, visit our website at wisdompubs.org.

If you would like to order a copy of our mail-order catalog, please contact us at:

Wisdom Publications

199 Elm Street

Somerville, Massachusetts 02144 USA

Telephone: (617) 776-7416 • Fax: (617) 776-7841

Email: sales@wisdompubs.org • www.wisdompubs.org

Wisdom Publications is a nonprofit, charitable 501(c)(3) organization affiliated with the Foundation for the Preservation of the Mahayana Tradition (FPMT).